FROM DULL TO DYNAMIC

TRANSFORMING YOUR PRESENTATIONS

STEPHEN D. BOYD

JOSHUA E. BOYD

Library of Congress Catalog   98-66422
ISBN   1-57097-391-7

Professional Press
Chapel Hill, NC 27515-4371

Manufactured in the United States of America

02 01 00 99 98   10 9 8 7 6 5 4 3 2 1

CONTENTS

POISE AND PROFESSIONALISM

SPECIFIC SPEAKING SITUATIONS

PREFACE

---•◆•---

We wrote this book to help people of all skill levels improve their presentations. As trainers, teachers, and speakers, we wanted to share some practical pointers that we have developed during a combined total of 40 years in the speaking business. We hope that you will find the instruction and examples in this book both interesting and immediately useful.

We, Josh and Steve, thank our wives Gina and Lanita for their encouragement, suggestions, and understanding during the challenges involved in the process.

We thank our readers, Bill Arnold, Dave Bryant, Jim Cassity, Linda Johnson, N. Edd Miller, and Ron Miller, for their valuable suggestions and reactions. We appreciate the hours of editing and typing Aaron Ellerbrook and Linda Dietz put into this book. We also thank our thousands of workshop participants and students whose feedback and participation helped us develop the approach to speaking presented in this book.

CONTENT AND SUPPORTING MATERIAL

DULL TO DYNAMIC

———◦•◦———

We have all been there, sitting in the audience while a speaker gently lulls us to sleep. Maybe we were required to attend the speech and had very little interest in the topic, or maybe we were very interested when the speech began. The presentation might even have information valuable to us, but for some reason, it's simply too boring for us to follow. We start working on something else or fighting sleep, hoping that the speaker at least be brief.

Maybe you have been in that same situation as the *speaker*, watching people nod off to sleep one by one, listening to only a smattering of polite applause at the end, facing few if any questions. Both are truly miserable experiences, and experiences like these make it no wonder people fear giving presentations so much.

But if you have ever been in the opposite situation, you understand the potential exhilaration of speaking. You have seen how a speaker, in just a few minutes, can capture an audience's attention, leaving audience members asking questions, thinking, and feeling excited about what they can do with the ideas they just received. Perhaps you have even been on the speaking end of such a presentation once or twice.

How can you reach this level of skill and maintain it time after time? What specific preparations distinguish a dull speaker from a dynamic speaker? This book will guide you through every phase of the speech—choosing your topic and gathering interesting support materials, organizing your ideas so that people can easily follow you from beginning to end, delivering the speech in a way that commands attention and response, polishing your visual aids and sense of presence, and handling specific speaking situations skillfully. You might not become a Churchill, a Reagan, or a Lincoln overnight, but you will be able to leave your days as a dull speaker behind in your transformation to a more dynamic presenter.

We believe presentation skills can be taught; speaking skill is not something decided at birth. Some people naturally possess a more outgoing personality or a stronger voice, but anyone can prepare, practice, and perform a presentation in an effective way that demands a response. Whether you speak in a business, educational, political, or religious context, this book teaches general principles you can use to become more dynamic.

Whether primarily informative or persuasive, all presentations seek a positive response. If they didn't, there would be no reason to give them. To make speaking worthwhile, people in your audience must have the power to make decisions based on what you say and whom you want to somehow influence. Thus any presentation, at some level, is a significant event—that is, someone in the room can act on your admonition to buy a million-dollar piece of equipment, or determine that the department or division will accept the proposal of your insurance company, or recognize the importance of your area of expertise and want to know more. When you speak, consider how you want audience members to respond, and then follow these guidelines to achieve that response.

Besides the obvious result of getting what you want by delivering a good presentation, developing speaking skills benefits you in other ways as well. In fact, few skills benefit you more in other areas of your life than the ability to speak well. Daniel Webster once said if all of his skills were taken away from him except one, the one he would want to retain would be the ability to speak, for with it, he could regain all the rest. Brock Bower, a writer for *Life* magazine, wrote, "It isn't always but every great leader has had eloquence—Lincoln, Roosevelt, Gandhi in many tongues—and no leader can safely mumble in moments of crisis or of hope."

Presentation skills will benefit your career. The more successful you become in your occupation, the more you will be called upon to speak. Employers look for people who can communicate well. One writer stated, "The thirty minutes an executive spends on his or her feet formally presenting his or her latest project to corporate superiors are simply and absolutely the most important thirty minutes of that or any other managerial season. The game isn't show and tell; it's gladiator time, career death or career glory...." An applicant for a job at a major computer company found that the company's main interview requirement was to give a presentation on anything but computers.

Presentation skills help you in interpersonal communication skills also. Learning to organize your thoughts for a presentation gives you self-discipline in organizing your thoughts when you speak on the phone or person to person. Developing a habit of having a main point and getting to it clearly in a presentation will encourage you to get to the point more quickly when conversing with another person.

Improving your presentation skills increases your credibility with audience members even outside the speaking environment. People judge you by what you say and how you say it. They will draw conclusions not only about you but also about the organization you represent. If you deliver a well-supported, interesting speech that makes a clear point, people are going to perceive you and your organization as intelligent, competent, and stimulating. In essence, if you speak well, you get higher marks in all areas. A dynamic speaker is perceived to be a dynamic person. Do you want to be that person? Do you want to know what it means to see a speech as an opportunity and not a chore? Then read on.

PREPARING

———◆·◆———

"*Discovery consists of looking at the same things as everyone else and thinking something different.*"

—Albert Szent-Gyorgi

Speakers control much of their success before they ever get up to speak. The key to that success is preparation. If you are prepared, you will be successful; if you don't prepare, then you deserve to fail. Following a simple preparation process that begins well before the presentation date and involves much thought can help lead you to speaking success.

PICKING

Picking the right topic isn't going to guarantee a great speech, but it's an important start. Whether you are assigned a topic or you have complete control, the best choice of topic is one you get excited about. Don't choose a topic or perspective just because you think your audience will welcome it. If you aren't excited about your topic or argument, you cannot expect your audience to be excited.

PERUSING

If you give at least one speech a month, you should think of all your reading and listening time as general preparation time. If you always have your mind open to possible speech materials, you'll be more likely to pick up new and creative material for your presentation (See more about this in the chapter on finding stories). Nonfiction books are excellent sources for good ideas, and Steve has even found some great examples in taxis. Because taxi drivers often have only one speed—breakneck—his awareness level in taxicabs is often heightened. Like Steve, you may have your own unusual experiences with cab drivers that you could use in a speech someday.

PONDERING

Once you have chosen a topic that you feel good about, think about the subject for several days before you do anything else. Talk to others about your topic and get their reactions. Just letting the speech topic incubate helps you develop creative examples and connections. Avoid the temptation to write down every idea immediately; when you start writing things down, you become limited by the scope of what is on paper. Once you have pondered the topic for a while, however, then you are ready to write ideas down.

Piecing

As you write down ideas, look up sources, and remember things you have found in your perusing that might be useful, you will begin to see how the pieces of the puzzle fit together. You're not to the outlining stage yet, and you don't want to limit yourself too much by what you write down. You do, however, want to make sure you have enough pieces of information to put together a coherent speech. If a piece seems to be missing, find it. To fill in a missing piece, look in various resources for information that is current and useful to the audience you will be addressing. For example, if you have an article from a trade journal, a quotation from a newspaper clipping, an interview with an expert, and a personal experience with the topic, you probably have more material on a single point than you can use. From these, you can then choose the one or two best pieces of evidence. This scenario usually ensures high quality support for each part of your presentation.

Planning Ahead

A word of caution for this entire process: give yourself enough time to do the work. Your presentation will be significantly less developed if you cram for it. Much of the inspiration for a presentation comes from mulling it over. Just thinking about your topic as you drive to and from work in the days preceding the presentation will give you a range of ideas that you won't have when you are pressed for time and wait until the day before the speech to prepare. If you have lived with a topic for a while, it shows in the depth of your thinking. In fact, when you make time to go through all these preparation steps, you'll have more ideas than you can cover. This is a good problem to have—you can eliminate your mediocre material and use only the best ideas and examples.

PRACTICING

An entire chapter in this book is devoted to practicing your presentation once it's in outline form, but even before you get to that stage, your material benefits from practice. Some of your preparation time should be spent not in writing, but in talking to people and experimenting with speech ideas informally. Try out one of your examples as dinner conversation with a small group of associates or family members. Just going over the idea aloud and getting people's feedback will help you to decide if and how to use it. Based on these informal practices and the questions people ask you, you can add significant details that add depth to the material.

PARCELING POINTS

After you feel comfortable with your ideas and evidence for those ideas, begin to develop an outline. Here your puzzle begins to take shape. With a jigsaw puzzle, you begin by separating the edge pieces and assembling them first; with the speech, you begin to think of possible main points and arrange different supporting materials where they seem to fit. With some trial and error, you will begin to develop a clear picture as you put things together.

PRONOUNCING

Except on rare occasions when you need to give a manuscript speech, you should never write out your speech word for word. If you do, you tend to read it instead of delivering it. Keeping your speech in outline form and writing down your key ideas helps you to *deliver* the material rather than *read* it. Even though you have prepared carefully each idea you present, you want to sound and act spontaneous in your delivery. Use the time after each practice session for further preparation because you'll have fresh ideas about how to rearrange or otherwise modify your presentation. When you have to think as you practice from key words, you get your best ideas for revision.

Effective presentations are prepared with a lot of time and thought. If you constantly look for possible speech material and then take advantage of preparation time to ponder your topic and try out your ideas, your finished product will be much more polished when you finally come to the point of putting your ideas in presentation form.

SAVING GREAT IDEAS

F inding the right words for a particular presentation is challenging and frustrating. Whether the right words are your own or someone else's, they won't help you unless you can save them. To help you save your great ideas to use in preparing new presentations and improving old ones, keep an idea book. An idea book is simply a notebook you keep with you so that you can write down any great ideas or quotations that might prove useful to you later. The Russian czar who founded St. Petersburg, Peter the Great, had an idea book. Get into the habit of finding things to put into your own idea book.

One of the best ways to find material for your speeches is to borrow from other sources. As Michel de Montaigne stated, "I quote others only the better to express myself." But how do you find relevant quotations? First, let others know you are always looking for quotations and examples about your topic of expertise. People are generally willing to help, and e-mail has made it much easier to pass along stories or quotations.

Second, read a lot. One of the benefits of reading is you will sometimes find gems tucked away in a chapter of a biography or even a novel. The fact that Peter the Great used an idea book, for instance, came from Robert K. Massie's biography *Peter the Great*. *The Wall Street Journal* also contains useful stories and quotations. Whatever your primary area of expertise, probably at least one journal or magazine is connected to it. That publication can also provide a wealth of quotations that help you better express your ideas.

Eventually, you'll acquire twenty or thirty quotations that you can use in a variety of situations. They become staples for introductions and conclusions and also help support specific points.

FAVORITE QUOTATIONS

"The greatest problem in communication is the illusion that it has been accomplished."
—George Bernard Shaw

"One word may be effective, but no word is as effective as the rightly timed pause."
—Mark Twain

"Everyone should be quick to listen, slow to speak, and slow to become angry."
—James 1:19

"The ordinary speaker gets the audience to think highly of the speaker. The exceptional speaker gets the audience to think highly of themselves."
—Joel Weldon

Be sure to include the name of the source with the quotation.

Quotations can be used as startling statements to begin or end presentations. An appropriate quotation can help the audience remember a main point. A relevant statement from someone else can also leave the audience with something to think about in your exit line. Just remember: when someone says something better than you can, borrow it and use it in your presentation. The audience doesn't care if it came from you as long as it helps them remember one of your ideas.

Not only is the idea book an effective way to keep track of quotations from others when you first hear them or see them in print, it's also a place for you to write down your own great ideas. Some of your best ideas for an upcoming speech will come to you when you're not at your desk; use your idea book to capture those thoughts. You may or may not use the idea in your next speech, but the mental discipline of thinking and writing it down will help you continually think about ways to improve your presentations. Ideas you write down today might prove useful months or years down the line. As Jim Rohn wrote, "Rarely does a good idea interrupt you. You have to cultivate ideas." When you get an idea, write it down in your idea book.

Immediately after you give a speech, you often have some of your best ideas for improving your next presentation, either from your own reflection or from members of your audience. Keep those ideas in your notebook as well.

We became serious about writing down ideas in 1989, and we now have a total of twelve idea books. Our idea books stimulate us to think more when we aren't at our computers because we have a resource in which to record our ideas on the spot. If you keep your entries, you'll be fascinated to see what thoughts were important enough to write down six months ago or a year ago. When you are preparing a new speech or revising one you have given in some form several times, it is refreshing to go through your idea book and see what might add newness to the content of the speech.

In addition, both of us keep track of books read during each year. If we can't recall a particular book from which an idea came, reviewing the list sometimes reminds us of the source.

Share your ideas with someone regularly; this reminds you to keep the idea book current. And when you share ideas, you often get additional ones from the other person. As A. S. Gregg put it, "You have a shilling. I have a shilling. We swap. You have my shilling and I have yours. We are no better off. But suppose you have an idea and I have an idea. We swap. We have increased our stock of ideas 100 percent." In addition, when you have accumulated several idea books, take time to go back over idea book number one. What happened two years ago may today have very specific applications. Great presentations need great ideas. To make sure you have as many great ideas as possible when constructing your presentation, keep an idea book. Capture your own good ideas and the eloquence of others so that you can use them later.

Finding Stories And Making Them Yours

(Plus Some Free Samples)

———•◆•———

A udience members often ask, "Where do you get those great stories for your speeches?" There are various places you can find good material. The most important source is personal experience. The more experiences you have in any area of life, the more possibilities you have for stories to use in your speeches. Write down any unusual experience you have or witness so that you can use it later. For example, here is a story from our family outing in 1991.

> In attending our second Indianapolis 500
> mile race, we were seated in row one of turn
> one, where most of the action was. On lap
> 194, 485 miles into the race, Michael Andretti
> and Rick Mears were dueling for the lead
> when Mears passed on the right (the outside)
> to the audible gasps of the crowd. As a result,
> he was able to win the race—his fourth
> victory in fourteen years of running at India-
> napolis. After the race, a reporter asked
> Mears when the last time was he had passed
> on the right to win a race. He said, "That was
> the first time. I simply did what I had to do
> to win the race."

This story was put together from our personal observation
of this event and a newspaper account of the race. We use
it to support points about risk-taking or having a passion for
something in life. We were there, and we saw it happen.

You may have to keep some stories tucked away until you
find just the right point or speech for them. Consider the
story of the old Bradley barn. Lightning struck and de-
stroyed it in 1959. The barn was rebuilt by neighbors, and
in 1963, the barn was flattened by a tornado. The barn was
built back again on the same spot, and in early 1996,
smoking teenagers burned it to the ground. Now where do
you think the fourth barn was *not* built? The story has been
written down, and someday it will fit perfectly in a speech.

Remember the "idea book" for quotations and thoughts?
Write experiences in it that you have or witness as soon as

you can after they happen. This ensures accurate details and specific description. Each time you do this, you increase your resources for speeches.

A second major source for stories is the newspaper. Peruse daily newspapers, such as local dailies, *The Wall Street Journal*, and *USA Today*. Newspaper stories are usually short, with specific facts and statistics you can easily weave into your speech. Recently, the cover story in *USA Today* dealt with common causes of airline and train crashes. Such accidents are typically caused by human error involving communication breakdowns. The article contained at least three dramatic examples that could be easily incorporated into talks on communication.

An example of this is found in the story about the day Teddy Roosevelt was shot by a would-be assassin. He survived because, instead of entering his chest, the bullet was absorbed by a glasses case and a thick speech manuscript he carried in his coat pocket. The story is documented in *The New York Times* for that day in 1912. It can be used in telling about the importance of our speech and in adding a light touch to discussing the power of our words. The punch line is, "I'm not suggesting that what we say is a matter of life and death, but I do believe that our speech is important." Newspapers can be invaluable sources to the speaker for new stories or to verify details of old ones.

A third source for stories is an expert in a particular area. This might include simply senior citizens who have a lot of experiences that make them experts on life. Ask these people open-ended questions that will prompt examples from their work. For example, ask, "What is the most unusual thing that has happened to you in your career?" "What is the funniest thing that has happened to you in your life or work?" "What is the most important thing you have learned in your career?" These open-ended questions often stimulate great stories. One auctioneer, asked about the most unusual thing that had ever happened in one of his auctions, answered by telling a funny story about two bidders getting into such a fight over an antique doll that they started pulling the prized doll apart.

Books—especially nonfiction—also provide you with good stories. Jon Krakauer's *Into Thin Air*, for instance, a book about Mount Everest, has a wealth of stories about the history of the climb which could be used in future speeches. And while nonfiction business books can be helpful, stories are more likely to come from other types of nonfiction—biography, adventure, travel. The more you read, the more you not only find stories, but are reminded of your own similar experiences that might make for interesting speech support.

Finally, find stories by visiting the historically significant areas of our country and the world. Around state capitals, you can find biographies and history books that contain interesting information about the state you're in. The state capitol building in Baton Rouge, Louisiana, for instance, still has the elevator Huey Long marked for the governor only, as well as the bullet holes in the wall left by Long's assassin. In Fiji we learned about cannibal forks, hideous-looking implements that until the late nineteenth century Fijians used when eating human flesh. What a challenge it is to find just the right speech for that tidbit! Traveling and learning about different places provides you with many unusual stories.

SOURCES FOR STORIES AND QUOTATIONS

Bits and Pieces, 12 Daniel Road, Fairfield, NY 07004

Executive Speaker, The Executive Speaker Co., P.O. Box 292437, Dayton, OH 45429

The Executive Speechwriter Newsletter, Emerson Falls, St. Johnsbury, VT 05819

Quote Magazine, 5302 Derringer Rd., Box 815, Las Cruces, NM 88004

Sparks From the Anvil, Concord Industrial Park, Concordville, PA 19331

The Jokesmith, 44 Queen's View Rd., Marlborough, MA 01752

Once you find stories, how do you use them for greatest impact? Here are criteria for including stories in your presentation.

First, pick the right story for you. Use a personal experience that was meaningful or a story from someone else that really made an impression on you. The right story is one that clearly supports the point you are making and one you are excited about telling.

Second, be animated in relating the story. Use gestures to describe what you are telling. If you are telling a little boy story, show the audience how tall he is by holding your hand three feet off the ground. Reinforce your story highlights with gestures. Move toward the audience when you come to the climax of the story.

Third, be specific in delivering the story. Answer the questions who, what, when, where, and how. For example, don't just say, "Teddy Roosevelt was almost killed by an assassin's bullet." Instead, say, "In the Presidential Campaign of 1912, Teddy Roosevelt was about to deliver a campaign speech in Milwaukee. As he was leaving his hotel, a man leaped from the crowd of supporters and shot TR point blank in the chest...."

Fourth, have a clear sense of direction in telling the story. Don't get bogged down in details. A story should have a beginning, a middle, and an end. Make sure each detail and description is critical to the story. Try to keep the telling of the story under two minutes. The longer the story, the more powerful it had better be. The audience won't be happy if you take five minutes to tell a story that does not turn out to be very interesting or remarkable.

Fifth, always connect the story with the point you are making. You might use a summary statement, such as, "This story shows us that...", or, "As we see from the story...." Don't tell a story just for the sake of telling a story; make sure the story has a purpose in the speech. A good time to tell a story is after a technical section of your speech when the audience might be getting bored. A story is a good way to bring attention back to you. The story can add suspense and a human element to an otherwise technical presentation.

Here is a story from Steve's experience that illustrates several of the principles mentioned in this chapter.

A few years ago I was taking a cab from O'Hare Airport to downtown Chicago. As I got into the cab, I could tell it was very clean. The floor of the back seat was so clean you could eat lunch off it. So I told the cab driver how impressed I was with the cleanliness of his cab. He thanked me and said he felt great pride in his service as a cab driver and he worked hard to always have a clean cab. As we drove along he said, "Do you remember Sam Cooke?" I said, "Of course, he was one of my favorite singers in the 1960s." He said, "I was a backup singer for Sam Cooke! I'm the one who sang the high notes on 'Cupid.'" And then can you imagine what he did next? He sang "Cupid" for me. I have taken many cab rides in my life but never like the one given to me by the backup singer for Sam Cooke. He did not just give me a ride — he provided a memory!

This story illustrates several of the principles in this chapter. The experience delighted Steve as it happened, and he thoroughly enjoys telling it to audiences. He is able to recount several specific details about the story, including dialogue with the cab driver. He uses lots of animation as he describes the cleanliness of the car. He has made applications from the story to customer service, added value, and doing your best on the job.

Tell stories. Your speeches will be enhanced, and audiences will remember more of what you say when you support your ideas with stories.

HUMOR IN THE PRESENTATION:
FINDING IT

"There is no reason why a joke should not be appreciated more than once. Imagine how little good music there would be if, for example, a conductor refused to play Beethoven's Fifth Symphony on the ground that his audience might have heard it before."

—A.P. Herbert

People today expect humor everywhere, not only on television and in magazines, but also in the speeches they listen to. Even in strictly serious speeches, it behooves speakers to use a little humor. This doesn't require imitating David Letterman or Jay Leno, however, or being a hilarious person to begin with. Here you will learn how to find and develop humor you can use in your presentations.

Some speakers say, "I could never use humor in my speech; I just don't feel comfortable with it." With the right kind of preparation, however, almost any speaker can use humor well. Just like transitions or stories, humor simply provides speakers with a tool. As a tool, humor can fix many things. Appropriate humor relaxes an audience, makes an audience feel more comfortable listening to you, draws attention to the point you are making, and even breaks down barriers so that your audience is more receptive to your ideas. People find it harder to disagree when they are smiling. Because of the benefits of humor, it's worth a little effort to find humor you can use in speeches even if you don't think of yourself as a funny person. Here are some ways to improve your sense of humor and find humor to enhance your presentations.

First, take humor breaks. We take lunch breaks and coffee breaks, so why not take a humor break? Take time to read your favorite comic strip each morning. Our favorite cartoons over the years have included "Herman," "The Far Side," "Speed Bump," "Close to Home," and "Zits." Just checking them out each morning brings us dozens of smiles and laughs per year. Go to movies you think are funny. Subscribe to e-mail humor services. Associate with people who make you laugh. All of these humor breaks heighten your awareness of humor, so you will be more sensitive to humor that might be useful.

Second, learn to think funny about the serious. This doesn't mean you should joke about tragic things, but you should try to bring a lighter approach to those irritating people or events that can put you in a bad mood or leave you frustrated. A friend described problems in his family this way: "We have a hyper family. I have hypertension, my wife hyperventilates, my daughter is hypersensitive, and my son is hyperactive." All these things were true. By linking them under one name, though, he was able to poke fun at some of the frustrating elements in his life. When you have this mental set, you often find great material from your experiences to include in your next presentation.

Seeing your mistakes with a sense of humor is a great way to find unique material by thinking funny about the serious. As a minister, Steve performs a lot of marriage ceremonies, and one day he learned the value of simple language. When it came time to exchange rings, he asked (as he always did until that day), "Do you have tokens of your affection for each other?" The bride and groom both looked at him and shook their heads. The wedding had a rather low budget, so he assumed the couple must not have gotten rings. He proceeded with the ceremony and was about to pronounce them husband and wife when the groom interrupted with, "Uh, we've got rings...." At the time, the situation was awkward, but in retrospect it was pretty funny. It also encouraged him to change; he now asks simply, "Are there rings?"

Share something funny with someone else, and you will receive humor in return. Jesus said in the Bible, "Give, and it will be given to you. A good measure, pressed down, shaken together and running over, will be poured into your lap." This statement is particularly true when it comes to sharing humor with others—you often get back more than you give. Find a cartoon that relates to your work or social environment and cut it out. Put at the bottom of the cartoon, "I thought you would enjoy this," and sign your name. Send it out to relevant people or put it on the bulletin board. Wait to see what happens. People who haven't done so in a while will smile at you. Eventually you may even find that someone will send you a cartoon! At the very least, other people might follow your lead of posting humor or talking about funny things. You can be even more direct by simply asking people to tell you their funniest jokes or personal experiences.

Keep track of things you say that other people find really funny. Lipscomb University basketball coach Don Meyer sometimes makes a big show of checking or scratching off jokes in his notes depending on the response he gets during a speech, but that technique is even more useful in keeping track of witty thoughts for future use.

Another way to cultivate your sense of humor is to make laughter legal in your environment. A friend who really likes Halloween goes to work on that day dressed as Kermit the Frog. This guy is about six feet four inches tall and weighs less than 200 pounds. Picture him in a green leotard and flippers walking around the plant all day. His costume says more to his employees than simply, "I like Halloween." He is saying by his appearance and actions that he believes it is okay to laugh at work. By simply promoting an atmosphere that allows for humor, you make it easier to find and be comfortable using humor in your next presentation.

Follow a child around. Children are able to laugh easily and find humor in unexpected places. They say many funny things—Art Linkletter made a career out of this realization. Teachers are in the best jobs to enjoy the humor of children. One year Lanita, an elementary school teacher, had a student named Derek who caused all kinds of trouble. One day, she had about had it with Derek, so she took him out in the hall. She said, "Derek, today you have pulled Suzie's hair, you have stolen Jason's crayons, and you have scribbled on Becky's paper. What is your problem?" He looked up at her and said, "My problem is...I'm sitting in the middle of a bunch of tattletales." It was all she could do to maintain her composure. All sense of discipline left her, and she let him back into the room. Children not only inadvertently say funny things, they also ask questions that give us new perspectives. Sadly, we usually lose our childlike humor and even take away the sense of humor for the child. We say, "Wipe that smile off your face," or, "Get serious; now is no time to laugh." Let children be funny and be there to observe them when they are.

Personal experiences and conversations aren't the only sources for humor. You might watch your favorite comedian or sitcom with pencil and paper in hand. If you hear a funny punch line, think of a way you can relate it to your own experiences. You might also simply use the line as is and give the source credit. To find more "stock" kinds of jokes, pick up joke books in the bookstore and just leaf through them. You can determine by casually reading one or two pieces of humor on random pages whether books might contain something useful to you. Never pass a humor section in a bookstore without looking for something you might be able to use. Go through issues of *Vital Speeches*. Often if someone else has used a funny piece in a speech, it might work for you too. Go through the various humor sections in *Reader's Digests* of at least ten years ago. Don't use a recent issue because too many people have read or heard those stories; the same warning holds true for humor sections of other magazines, such as *Rotary*, *Kiwanis*, *Farm Journal*, and *Quote*. If you speak to religious groups, *The Door* has humorous material.

Once you have begun cultivating a sense of humor and using some of these techniques to find funny material, you will find humor everywhere. Once you have found it, commit yourself to be more interesting and effective by using humor in your presentations.

Here are stories we find funny. Feel free to adapt them to your own presentations.

HOW DID YOU DO THAT?

A magician was working on a cruise ship. He had a parrot that was always ruining his act, saying in the middle of his trick, "The card is up his sleeve," or "He has a dove in his pocket," or, "He slipped it through a hole in his hat."

One day the ship sank. The parrot and the magician found themselves together on a life raft. For several days, the parrot sat silent and stared at the magician. On the fourth day, the parrot said, "Okay, I give up. What did you do with the ship?"

THE FIREMEN

One evening as two firemen sat outside the local volunteer fire department in Gobbler's Knob, Tennessee, one asked, "Did you hear about that big fire in Texas?"

"Yeah, it's a big one, ain't it? We ain't never seen nothing like that."

"No, when old Junior's barn burned down, that was a big one, but it was about the biggest we ever put out."

"You know, I bet we could put that oil well fire out."

So they jumped into the fire truck; they drove down to Texas; they reached the oil fields; they drove through the gate, didn't slow down, and drove smack into the middle of the fire. They jumped down from the truck, pulled off their yellow firemen's coats, and beat the fire out. The company had a big celebration and a press conference. As the C.E.O. presented a $500,000 check to Jake, the fire chief, he asked, "What are you going to do with all of this money, Jake?"

Jake replied, "Well, the first thing we're gonna do is fix the brakes on that truck!"

TRAFFIC

"Your driver's license says you should be wearing glasses," the traffic cop said to the speedster. "Why aren't you wearing them?"

"I have contacts," the speedster said.

"I don't care who you know," the cop said. "You're getting a ticket anyway."

QUOTABLE QUOTE

Willie Sutton, one of the most famous bank robbers of the twentieth century, was the subject of numerous books, a TV drama, and at least one song. He was also a favorite of newspaper reporters, who could count on him for the kind of quote that makes a headline bounce.

Sutton had spent most of his adult life in prison. Though he escaped more than once, his short bursts of freedom always ended with an arrest for bank robbery. In an attempt to learn why he continued along such a futile course, one reporter asked, "Willie, why do you keep robbing banks?"

"Because," Sutton said smoothly, "that's where the money is."

LOOKING FOR ME

A man dialed the phone number of his client. The phone was picked up with barely enough time for it to ring. "Hello?" a small boy's voice answered.

"Hi. Is your mom home?"

"Yes, but she is busy," the little boy replied.

"How about your dad?"

Again the little boy said, "He is busy, too."

The man then asked, "Is there any adult there that I can talk to?"

"Yes," said the boy. "A policeman, but he is busy."

"Anyone else?"

"A fireman, but he is busy, too."

Concerned, the man asked, "What are all those people doing at your house?"

The little boy answered, "Looking for me."

EGGS

One day a Baptist minister found a shoe box in the back of his wife's closet. When he opened it, he found $1,000 in cash and three eggs. When his wife came home, he confronted her with the box and asked her what it meant.

She explained that since their marriage began, each time she heard him give a bad sermon she put an egg in the box. He did some quick figuring and realized that over the past 25 years she must have heard thousands of sermons. He decided that three eggs was pretty good.

The he remembered the $1,000 in cash. She hugged him and said, "Well, whenever I got a dozen eggs, I sold them!"

PERSUASION

"There are advantages and disadvantages about this property," said the honest real estate agent. "To the north is the gas works, to the east is a glue factory, to the south a fish and chips shop, and to the west a sewage farm. Those are the disadvantages."

"What are the advantages?" asked the prospective buyer.

"You can always tell which way the wind is blowing," said the agent.

WAKE UP CALL

A family was staying at a motel. The wife had awakened early and started packing the bags and carrying them to the car. Returning from a trip to the auto, she accidentally walked into the wrong room. Seeing a man lying in bed, she assumed it was her husband and shouted at the top of her voice, "Get out of that bed!" Suddenly realizing her mistake, she turned and ran. As she left the room she heard the man saying, "Boy, that sure is some wake-up service."

THE FUNERAL OF A SAINT

Two mean brothers lived in a certain city in Mississippi. They were bad folks, never had anything to do with the church. One of those mean brothers died, and the other brother went to the local preacher. "I want you to preach at my brother's funeral. And during the funeral service, if you call my brother a saint, I'll give you $5,000."

"All right," the preacher said, "I'll do that. The church needs $5,000." The preacher got up and said, "Ladies and gentlemen, the man in this casket we're buryin' here today has got to be the most vile, meanest, low down-est scoundrel I have ever known in my life. But compared to his brother sitting right over there, this man was a saint."

LAST NAME ONLY

The manager of a large office noticed a new man one day and told him to come into his office. "What is your name?" was the first thing the manager asked the new guy.

"John," the new guy replied.

The manager scowled, "Look...I don't know what kind of namby-pamby place you worked before, but I don't call anyone by their first name. It breeds familiarity and that leads to a breakdown in authority. I refer to my employees by their last names only...Smith, Jones, Baker...that's all. I am to be referred to only as Mr. Robertson. Now that we got that straight, what is your last name?"

The new guy sighed, "Darling. My name is John Darling."

"Okay, John, the next thing I want to tell you is...."

HUMOR IN THE PRESENTATION:

USING IT

———◦•◦———

*"When the mouth is open for laughter, you may
be able to shove in a little food for thought."*

—Virginia Tooper

Once you develop a sense of humor, you are well on your way to developing presentations that hold people's interest and make points in memorable ways. Constructive use of humor in presentations depends on several keys.

First, after you have written down or accumulated some material that has potential, make sure the humor is funny to you before you use it. If you don't laugh or smile when you go back and read the cartoon, joke, pun, or whatever it is, then you certainly can't expect an audience to be amused. Only use material that makes you laugh, not just anything that seems to relate well to your topic. Figure out what kind of humor makes you laugh and use it. For example, some speakers feel more comfortable including a story with a punch line, so they look for longer jokes rather than puns or one-liners. What cartoons make you laugh? Which comedians are your favorites? What television sitcoms do you enjoy most? The answers to these questions give a good picture about the humor you are attracted to. If you think something is really funny, you are more likely to make it funny to your audience.

Second, before using humor in your speech, try it out with small groups of people. Share your story or one-liner with the family at dinner or your co-workers at lunch. Do they seem to enjoy it? Even if your experimental group doesn't laugh or smile initially at something you find funny, keep experimenting. The problem might be in the way you are delivering the joke or quip. It might take several retellings of the humor to find the right pacing, or pauses, or vocal quality. It might take several retellings to tighten the language and choose just the right words to get the best response. Take this clumsy example: "Life insurance is something you never need again if you don't have it when you need it, like a parachute." Compare that line to this from Joe Taylor Ford: "Life insurance is like a parachute— if you ever need it and don't have it, you'll never need it again!" Practice with a humorous tidbit several times before you decide to discard it. If other people consistently find something funny, only use it in a speech after you are comfortable telling it from memory.

Third, use humor if it relates to a point you are making. Don't use humor that is simply there to make the audience laugh—you might call this "gratuitous humor." People might laugh heartily at your humor but not understand the point it makes in your speech. Humor with no point can even cause audiences to remember less of the substance of your speech because they see the joke as a separate entity and try to remember it to tell their friends. If the humor ties in with your point, however, the audience will more than likely remember both. If you find a really funny story, look at it from all angles to see if you can fit it to your point. Only when you have thought of a connection should you use the humor.

Fourth, choose humor from your own experience as much as possible. You don't have to worry that people have heard it before, and you will feel more comfortable telling something that has actually happened to you. You can only do this, of course, if you are careful to record your funny experiences in an idea book. Here's an example: Steve was making a bank deposit one day at a drive-in window. When he asked to make a second deposit, the teller said (with a straight face), "I'm sorry, you'll have to go around the bank a second time to make a second deposit." We both laughed, and we have a line to work into a presentation.

Fifth, use visual humor. You might find a prop that would be humorous. For example, when Steve speaks to high school students, he likes to take one of his old shirts and cut out most of the chest area, leaving only the sleeves, the collar, and the center placket. He then buttons his coat so that the shirt looks normal. He tells them that he often has a problem with shirt collars and cuffs wearing out quickly, and when he bought this shirt, it had a lifetime guarantee on the cuffs and collar. He says although the guarantee was true, the shirtmaker neglected to do as well with the rest of the shirt—and he opens his coat to a lot of laughter. In addition to homemade props like this, you can look in magic shops or toy stores for gimmicks or simple tricks that might work as funny pieces in your speech. We often use a basic rope trick for a light piece. It took us only about an hour to learn the trick, but it has evoked hundreds of smiles and laughs since.

Is there anything unusual about your appearance that you might poke fun at? Steve has a crooked little finger from which he gets a lot of mileage at his own expense. Josh likes to wear bow ties, and he jokes about the special benefits of wearing bow ties. Remember—don't poke fun at someone else if you can use yourself instead.

Sixth, begin with something short to develop your confidence. You might start by summarizing a cartoon and its caption, or you might simply show the cartoon on the overhead projector. This approach reduces the pressure to be funny because the outcome of the humor is based on the cartoon, not you. You might try a pun or a one-liner as well, but be aware a favorable response to a pun is usually a groan, not a laugh. With all of these, the time investment is small, and an audience won't be terribly disappointed if your attempt at humor is not very funny. Whatever type of humor you use, always try to condense it; conciseness and brevity are assets to any humor. Be particularly careful about launching into a long humorous story—audiences are quick to forgive a single line that may not be funny, but they don't have much patience with a long anecdote that just isn't worth the lame punch line. The longer your humor is, the funnier it had better be. Start small and build your confidence before striking out into lengthier kinds of humor.

Funny experiences come from times when the ordinary turns into new challenges like trying to drive a rental car in Australia. Driving on the left side of the road with the steering wheel on the right side of the car created a lot of confusion for Steve—and entertainment for the family members in the car. He tells this story: When he wanted to turn right, he found himself turning on the windshield wipers. The way he learned to cope was just to quit signaling altogether! Shifting gears was even worse, for he tended to want to turn on the emergency brake. He has since applied this anecdote to taking risks or to the importance of teamwork, since it took other members of the family to keep him informed of traffic signs and other cars as he attempted to negotiate driving the car under unusual conditions for him.

In addition to the caution about starting small with humor, heed other warnings about the use of humor also. Don't use off-color jokes or jokes that poke fun at things people cannot change—especially nationality, ethnicity, or sex. Never use profanity in your humor. Don't tell sexist jokes. Don't preface your material by saying, "This is a funny story." What if you tell it and no one laughs? If you haven't set the audience up to expect something funny, people will take it as a serious story, and you will be off the hook for the humor part. And if people don't laugh at something you expected them to laugh at, just move on to the next point—excuses only prolong something that already hasn't worked. Avoid old stories. How do you know if a story is old? Try it out on several people similar to those who will be in your audience, and you will soon know. Remember, even if you have heard it for a long time, a story isn't old if your audience hasn't heard it.

Here are some examples of various types of humor presenters commonly use.

1. PERSONAL EXPERIENCE. This personal experience can be used to talk about positive language: Driving down the interstate one day, Steve saw a trucker who had a great sense of humor. Signs were on the back of the truck with an arrow pointing to each side. The one on the left said, "El Paso," and the one on the right said, "El Cruncho."

2. PUN. Two men were walking through the zoo. One was a visitor from the Czech Republic. The two stopped to admire the bears. Suddenly, one of the bears reached out, grabbed the Czech, and promptly ate him. The other man ran to the warden crying, "The bear! It ate my friend!" "Calm down, sir. I'll get your friend back for you," said the warden. "Just tell me, was it the male bear that ate him or the female bear?" "I think it was the male bear." So the warden got his

gun and shot the male bear. However, when they opened up the dead bear, there was no sign of the victim. "Oh, no!" cried the man. "It must have been the female who ate him up!" So the warden shot the female and sure enough, the Czech was inside. The moral of the story? Never trust anyone who says the Czech is in the male!

A scientist made a clone of himself perfect in every way except it had a foul mouth. At first, the scientist thought he could deal with it, but as time went on, the clone became more and more profane until the scientist could handle it no longer. He took his clone on a trip to the Grand Canyon, and when the clone wasn't expecting it, the scientist pushed it over the side to its death. Unfortunately for the scientist, however, another tourist witnessed this and the park police arrested him. The charge? Making an obscene clone fall.

3. DELIVERY. Sometimes the delivery alone makes something funny, particularly when caricaturing someone. Dana Carvey's impression of President Bush was funny not necessarily because of what he said, but because the way he said it emphasized some of Bush's mannerisms. Red Skelton is another comedian who was funny because of the different characters, such as Clem Kadiddlehopper, he developed primarily with delivery and facial expression.

4. ONE-LINER. Journalist Ambrose Bierce wrote that a connoisseur is a specialist who knows everything about something and nothing about anything else.

5. JOKE. A man tells a friend, "Have you heard the story about the dirty window?" "No," said his friend. "Well, you couldn't see through it anyway." The friend likes the story, so he goes home to repeat it to his wife. "Have you heard the story about the window you couldn't see through?" "No," she replied. "Well, it's too dirty to tell anyway."

6. EXAGGERATION (HYPERBOLE). In writing workshops, Josh uses humor to help explain why, contrary to what people might have heard, it's sometimes appropriate to end a sentence with a preposition. When Winston Churchill was criticized for ending a sentence with a preposition, he responded, "That, sir, is the sort of arrant pedantry up with which I will not put."

7. CARTOON. A good cartoon takes the pressure to be funny off of you. If you can find one that makes your point well, a cartoon is a good way to begin using humor.

Think of humor as a tool that improves your presentation just as attention-getting devices and smooth transitions do. Humor is simply another way of making a point with your audience. And by making your content more enjoyable, it can help you be a more effective speaker. Remember the saying, "A smile is a curve that straightens out a lot of things."

Don't Count
Your Chickens:
Using Statistics
And Analogies

S tatistics and analogies are important types of support, but they often are used inappropriately.

One major problem with statistics is speakers often use too many of them. The key to effective statistics in a speech is to use them sparingly. Don't complicate matters by giving six different numbers in a row. Your audience will leave you quickly—mentally if not physically.

When using statistics, it's vitally important to keep current on your research. Make sure you have the most recent statistics on your topic. Books are often poor sources for statistics because they may be out of date by the time the book is published, so journals or magazines would be more current. Round off statistics when appropriate. Telling your audience there are 2,320,732 ratchets may be tedious to the ears. Instead say there are more than 2 million ratchets available. Use statistics in combination with other evidence or support. Apply them after you have given a story, definition, or explanation, and always give the source. This adds credence to the number as well as reinforcing your credibility. When possible, demonstrate the statistic with a chart or graph. Helping your audience visualize the number gives it more impact to prove your point.

Analogies paint pictures for your audience. An analogy is simply an extended comparison. Instead of comparing two items in one way, the analogy may draw connections in five, six, or seven ways. You can build the analogy to fit the specific situation. However, incorporating analogies brings problems as well as benefits. At some point the analogy will break down. Just because two things are alike in four or five ways doesn't necessarily mean they will be alike in the sixth or seventh way. Thus you should never try to prove a point using the analogy. If members of your audience don't accept your point, they will zero in on the analogy to show how your proposal is invalid because the analogy will break down at some point. Instead use the analogy to help explain your point. The analogy is a great way to make your point memorable. A good analogy will cause audience members to take the point with them after the speech has long been over.

General reminders about the use of the analogy are the following: Keep your analogy short. It's easy to get caught up in your analogy and lose sight of the purpose for using it in the first place. Keep organization tight. Be careful to draw a specific conclusion from the analogy. Because the analogy can go in so many directions, your audience may think in a tangent that you didn't intend unless you finish by specifying the conclusion from the analogy. Don't say, "I'm going to give you an analogy." Just speak it.

Unlike stories or description, statistics and analogies may not be needed for every speech. But when needed, these two types of support can have an impact on your audience.

PRESENTATIONS ARE BUILDINGS:

USING METAPHORS

"The greatest thing by far is to have a command of the metaphor....It is the mark of genius, for to make a good metaphor implies an eye for resemblances."

—Aristotle

An effective presentation requires a great deal of planning. In the beginning of the speech, a speaker must lay a strong foundation for what will follow, and the speech must have good structure for it to stand. If any of these supports are missing, the whole thing will collapse.

The preceding paragraph is a brief example of how metaphors structure our thinking. By taking a simple metaphor, such as "presentations are buildings," and then using the terms "structure," "lay a strong foundation," and "collapse" to continue that metaphor, a speaker can direct audience members' thinking more precisely in the intended direction. Most people's idea of a metaphor is what they learned in school—a metaphor is a comparison not using "like" or "as." That definition certainly still holds true, but this chapter deals with using metaphor in a more strategic and extended way than, "That baby is an angel."

Using an extended metaphor throughout a speech works even more powerfully than a standard analogy because it's more subtle—two writers used the term "metaphorical fusion" to describe its effect.[1] To achieve the powerful reinforcement of metaphor, you must first choose a metaphor your audience understands. Usually, metaphors tap into very simple concepts: "business is war." "This company is a family." For a particular audience, though, your metaphor might be more specific: at an engineering company, you might use the metaphor "business is a circuit." Whatever your metaphor, it needs to be understood easily by your audience.

Not only must the metaphor be understandable, it must achieve the tone you want to communicate. This is metaphor's greatest strength, but it also presents the biggest challenge—choosing an appropriate metaphor. To see how

---

[1] Chaim Perelman and L. Olbrechts-Tyteca, *The New Rhetoric*, trans. John Wilkinson and Purcell Weaver (Notre Dame, IN: U of Notre Dame P., 1969): 401.

different metaphors create different tones, consider the metaphors several CEOs used to talk about downsizing in their corporations in the early 1990s. A new CEO at a struggling computer company used a surgery metaphor for downsizing, saying he wasn't going to keep "slicing" or making "mindless, meat-axe cuts," but he wanted to "stop the bleeding" in order to get the company "back on its feet." This surgery metaphor indicates the process would be painful but careful, and the process is absolutely necessary to restore the company's "health." In contrast (and in choosing a metaphor understandable to his audience), the CEO of a defense contractor used the metaphor, "workforce reduction is survival of the fittest." He urged the company to be "more fiercely competitive," "lean and smart," continuing a "constant struggle" to be a "survivor." This metaphor is again fiercer than simply getting in shape, indicating hard times ahead because the goal isn't to thrive, but more basically to survive. It also sounds a bit less sensitive to employees than the careful "surgery" metaphor. In another approach, the CEO at a large consumer products company used the metaphor, "downsizing is getting in shape." This metaphor was reflected in his call to "reduce layers," "slim down," and become "leaner, faster, and more flexible." This metaphor implied increased efficiency and harder work by everyone, but not as many drastic measures as surgery or a battle for survival.

As these examples illustrate, a third key to using metaphor effectively is to use a variety of words and phrases that reinforce the metaphor *without* simply repeating the metaphor over and over. When an Indiana utility tried to prevent an unwanted takeover by another power company, it used the metaphor "a corporate takeover is war." But rather than simply repeat that phrase, company officials spoke about the other company wanting to "raid the pockets" of Indiana electric consumers, calling it a "legal assault...being waged." A consumer group said, "the first battle has been fought" and the bidding company could not "win a war with its own customers." In this case, the audience for the metaphor (shareholders who would vote whether to accept the unsolicited offer) acted in the way the metaphor suggested: they "defended" their company by refusing the offer.

So the next time you want to set a specific tone in your speech, think about an appropriate metaphor you can invoke several times during your speech. Do you want to admonish a sales force to work harder to take market share from competing firms? You might use the "business is a game" metaphor. Tell sales team members they have to be more "competitive" in order to "win" market share away from the "competition." Give them "targets" or "goals" they can "aim" at in order to "beat" the "competition." Even though you might never actually utter the words "business is a game," your point will be unmistakable. An extended metaphor for your presentation takes a little more planning, but it can make a big difference in "constructing" a powerful appeal.

ORGANIZATION

ATTENTION FACTORS

———◆———

"That which attracts attention determines action."

—William James

It is one thing to get your audience's attention at the beginning of a speech, but it's quite another to maintain the audience's attention for the whole twenty or thirty minutes of your presentation. Speakers fear putting people to sleep with their presentations, but they actually have some control over whether that happens. Here are some ways of holding the attention of your audience:

1. **Reveal the structure of your presentation at the beginning.** Tell the audience in the first minute your speech will have three points. Preview them and then occasionally summarize what you have said. Structure makes it easier for people to follow along. People stop listening quickly, however, when they don't see a plan in your speech.

2. **Use suspense**. If you can build to a climax by revealing information little by little, you stand a better chance of keeping the audience with you. Reveal a visual aid a little at a time. Describe a case study and then give the startling conclusion later in the speech.

3. **Tell stories to illustrate a point**. People cannot help but pay attention when the speaker begins a story: "On my way to work yesterday as I was driving along I-71, I saw a...." We like adult versions of "Once upon a time...." Support or illustrate technical information with stories. Stories make a speech come alive for your audience.

4. **Use a lively delivery style**. Move out from behind the lectern at least once during the speech. Take a step occasionally toward the audience to emphasize a point. Build into your presentation content that demands gestures to describe a picture or reinforce a point. Movement attracts attention, so be animated with your face and gestures.

   The voice also affects delivery. It can be used to bring attention back to the speaker because pausing for effect gets attention. Remember in grade school when the teacher would suddenly stop talking? Everyone looked up and wondered what the teacher was going to say next. You can get that same response in a speech by using pauses to draw attention to important ideas. Another way to make key points is to punch out proper nouns with extra force. The rise and fall of the voice keeps people listening. A quick way to make the audience stop listening is to launch into a monotone pitch.

5. **Solicit audience participation**. A simple audience participation technique is to take an informal survey; ask for a show of hands in response to a question that relates to your topic. You might also do something that requires an audience volunteer. If one audience member is standing up in front of the group, everyone feels involved. Anything that requires an audience to be involved with the speaker is effective in bringing attention back to you as the speaker. Johnny Carson had the gimmick of saying, "It was so hot...," and then pausing for the audience to respond with, "How hot was it?" Johnny then launched into a series of one-liners. You might also have the audience say something in unison or even write down a key idea you want people to remember.

To hold attention, reveal the structure of your speech, use suspense, tell stories, develop an animated delivery, and involve the audience. In most presentations you want your audience to do something or to believe something, and maintaining attention is a necessary means to either of these ends.

THREE POINTS AND A POEM:

STRUCTURING THE PRESENTATION

———◦•◦•◦———

"The ability to express an idea is well nigh as important as an idea itself."

—Bernard Baruch

People in your audience pay better attention and remember more of your message if they can see a clear structure to your presentation. Structure not only arranges things in a way that makes them easy to follow, it appeals to us at a very basic level—humans need structure. Even for the messiest of us, there comes a day when we feel the need to straighten our desks! You might have the most powerful material in the world, but if it's jumbled and difficult to follow, the point of your message will be lost. As a speaker, you need to demonstrate from the beginning a structure that makes it easy for the audience to understand your ideas.

First, use the point and support approach. This satisfies both left-brained and right-brained members of your audience. The right-brained person is looking for support that connects with the emotions, and the left-brained audience member looks for support that clearly backs up the point. State your point and then give your story or other kind of evidence that supports the point, and you meet the needs of both kinds of audience members. The pattern for conciseness is a point and support, a point and support.

Second, remember Shakespeare's words: "Brevity is the soul of wit." Never take ten minutes to make a point if you can just as easily do it in five. When you are concise, people see you as sharp, intelligent, and in control. Revise stories so that you can tell them in as few words as possible. Eliminate details that are unimportant to the point of the story. The shorter you can make a story, the more impact it will have. Can you use fewer statistics and still make your point? Are all your explanations necessary, or is there any knowledge you think your audience will already have? People stay with and respond best to concise and straightforward material.

Check your conciseness by counting your points and supporting materials. You should have few points and much support. In a typical twenty-minute presentation, for instance, you might have three points with several pieces of evidence for each. When you tell an audience, "I am going to make seven points," you admit that you have no idea how to be concise. One of the reasons for Woodrow Wilson's failure to secure American support for a League of Nations after World War I might just have been his *14* points; who can remember that many? People have enough trouble with Moses's *Ten* Commandments! You should always be able to condense your presentation to five main points or less.

A third way to become better organized is to use transitions that give a sense of direction from point to point. Even a simple one-word signpost like "first" or "second" makes listeners feel there is planned, directed movement in your presentation. Internal summary is another transition that demonstrates direction as it helps you make your structure clear. Internal summary simply tells your audience where you have been and where you are going: "Now that we have talked about clarity, let's move on to conciseness." To stay focused and use your time most efficiently, give your message direction by using transitions.

A fourth way to demonstrate organization is to use the number three. As long ago as Robert of Basevorn in 1322, speakers have recognized the special nature of the number three in western culture. For some reason, people have long tended to remember and respond best to things grouped in threes, so when possible, have three points. Build a point on three pieces of evidence. Use a list of three items in an illustration. Audiences will remember more easily content grouped in threes, and the self-discipline of limiting yourself to three will force you to be concise.

A fifth way to a well-organized presentation is the tool of repetition. To help people stay with you and remember important points, repeat key ideas. You might do this as you finish a point (with an internal summary), or you might even pause and then restate a highly significant point.

A sixth way to help people follow your structure is to preview your main points. After you have the attention of audience members at the beginning, tell them what you plan to do in the presentation. Audiences feel more at ease with speakers when they know what the speeches are going to do. A preview might include listing your main points, or it might simply involve telling your audience what the main idea is that your main points will support. You might say, "Today I want to cover these three points...", or, "When I finish this presentation, you will understand that...", or, "If you get nothing else out of this speech, I want you to remember that...." Any of these previews will prepare the audience to follow the rest of the presentation. The preview is also helpful because it forces you to decide what the most important parts of your presentation are. Remember the old saying, "If it is foggy in the pulpit, it is cloudy in the pew." If you as the speaker are not clear about what you are doing, then the audience is certainly going to have a difficult time following what you say.

Good speakers must be organized and concise. The old preacher's formula of "three points and a poem" might not always be the best structure for you, but any good structure gives the audience a clear sense of direction and connects points to supporting material. And if you use a variety of evidence but clearly connect it all to your main theme, you will satisfy both left-brained and right-brained listeners.

MAKING THE FIRST
TWO MINUTES COUNT

In the movie *A Fish Called Wanda*, Kevin Kline's character always asked people to repeat the middle of what they just said. Like him, most people remember best what you say first and last. To the speaker, this means the introduction and the conclusion are crucial to the overall success of a speech.

The introduction should do three things: seize attention, provide a preview, and establish rapport. The most important of these is to seize the audience's attention. Just because the audience is looking at you doesn't mean listening is taking place. Your first couple of minutes must win the attention of audience members so that they want to listen to the rest of your presentation.

A variety of ways can be used to get attention. Begin with a startling statement or an unusual statistic. *Wall Street Journal* writer Stephen Moore, discussing government spending, noted that using the $2.5 trillion federal, state, and local government spends each year, a person could buy all the farmland in the U.S. and all the stock of the 100 most profitable U.S. corporations, with money left over. With a surprising beginning like that, an audience wants to hear more.

Another way of getting attention is to tell a story. Whether the story is something you find or something that actually happened to you, you can't beat it for making a point and maintaining attention.

You could also ask a question to gain attention for your focus. "How many of you had breakfast this morning?" might be a good way to start a talk on nutrition. Even a rhetorical question can work. "How many of you would like to have a million dollars?" A rhetorical question like this doesn't need an overt response, yet it can move the thinking of the audience in the direction of an investment or financially-related topic.

Using a visual aid or giving something away can also bring the audience's attention to you. When speaking about creativity, for instance, Blow Pops can be given away as an illustration—it took a pretty creative person to think about putting gum and candy together on a stick, but today almost everyone has at least tried that simple invention.

A relevant quotation can also grab attention. To introduce a speech about listening, you might relate the proverb about how our physical features stress the importance of listening: we have two ears on the sides of our head, visible to everyone, and only one tongue, which is placed in a cage behind ivory bars.

After getting attention, introductions should preview what will happen in the rest of the speech. The preview might state the focus of the presentation or the main points you plan to cover in the presentation. However you do this, you want to let the audience know what to expect in your speech. Continuing a speech on listening, the speaker might say, "I will give you three ways to improve your listening skills: ask questions, concentrate on the talker, and eliminate distractions."

Introductions also establish rapport between you and the audience. Getting attention and letting the audience know what is going to happen in the speech help develop rapport, but you should also be pleasant and show you are interested in talking to your particular audience in the introduction. Smiling, being enthusiastic, and demonstrating knowledge of your audience will contribute to an audience's comfort level with you.

A strong introduction seizes attention, previews the presentation, and establishes rapport with the audience. A good introduction also gives you a positive start you can then build on in the rest of your speech. If you memorize only one part of your speech, the first few lines are a wise choice.

Earning The Right To Sit Down

———◆———

Though the introduction is important, your conclusion acts as the other bookend that holds up your speech. Your job isn't finished when you get through the body of the speech; your conclusion must be memorable. One challenge in a conclusion is how to lead into it smoothly while still forewarning the audience that you are almost finished. Prepare the audience for your ending. When people know you are getting to your last words, they are more likely to pay close attention. Saying "In conclusion,..." isn't the smoothest way to do this. It is abrupt and a little clumsy, and other approaches make such a phrase unnecessary. Instead of being this obvious, show that you are about to conclude in other ways. A change in manner can accomplish this very easily. Pause and look around the room. Step away from the lectern. Begin a summary. All of these things indicate a change and alert people that you are almost finished without beating them over the head with "In conclusion,...."

A MEMORABLE CONCLUSION SHOULD...

1. Summarize main points.

2. Move the audience to change.

3. End with a strong exit line.

Once you have moved into your ending, three things can ensure that the audience will leave with a positive reaction to your speech. First, summarize what has been said in the main part of your presentation. Doing this reminds your audience members what you want them to remember. On the listening topic, you might say, "So we can see that by following these three simple points, we can improve our listening significantly."

Second, move people to belief or to action. Before people can change as you want them to, they must be told exactly what you want them to do. "To become a better listener I urge you to work on specific principles that we have discussed today. Remember to ask questions and paraphrase what the speaker has said."

The third key to concluding is a strong exit line. This can be a fitting quotation or a carefully created line that gives the audience something to think about and earns you the right to sit down. Simply trailing off, saying, "I guess that's about it," or mumbling "Thanks" doesn't do this. In old western movies, the last frame would show the cowboy riding off into the sunset, followed by big bold letters proclaiming, "THE END." This belabored the obvious. Comparable to that is the speaker who ends with "Thank you" or "Thanks for your attention," which is not as much a show of appreciation as it is the announcement, "I'm finished and I'm going to my seat." This kind of weak ending might lessen your audience's opinion of your entire speech. A strong exit line, however, is a way to end on a strong note and add a touch of class to the speech. Some of the most memorable quotations in our culture, in fact, began as well-crafted exit lines.

GREAT EXIT LINES

"I know not what course others may take; but as for me, give me liberty, or give me death!"

—Patrick Henry,
1775 speech to the
Virginia Convention

"With malice toward none, with charity for all, with firmness in the right as God gives us to see the right, let us strive on to finish the work we are in, to bind up the nation's wounds, to care for him who shall have borne the battle and for his widow and his orphan, to do all which may achieve and cherish a just and lasting peace among ourselves and with all nations."

—Abraham Lincoln,
Second Inaugural Address

"For many are called, but few are chosen."

—Jesus,
concluding the parable
of the wedding feast

"From every mountainside, let freedom ring, and when this happens...when we allow freedom to ring, when we let it ring from every village and every hamlet, from every state and every city, we will be able to speed up that day when all of God's children, black men and white men, Jews and Gentiles, Protestants and Catholics, will be able to join hands and sing in the words of the old Negro spiritual, 'Free at last! Free at last! Thank God Almighty, we are free at last!'"

—Martin Luther King, Jr.,
"I Have a Dream" speech

"May you never sell yourself at discount prices, and may you always go for the high bid!"

—Steve Boyd,
"High Bid" Speech

Even if you speak from key word notes, you should plan the specific wording of your exit line in advance. This exit line could be a one-sentence synopsis of the main point of your speech. It could be an admonition to your audience. It could even include a fitting quotation. Whichever type of exit line you choose, it should relate to your main point and give closure to the speech—no one should wonder whether or not you are finished. With the listening speech you might close with, "In the words of listening consultant Ron Meiss, 'Hearing happens; listening is a choice.'" Another option would be to say, "Long ago the master communicator Jesus Christ said, 'He that hath ears to hear, let him hear. And to him that hears, more shall be given.'"

If you choose to memorize just two things in your presentation, learn the opening words and the closing words. Audiences remember best what you say first and last, and a strong conclusion sends people away thinking about the message you have given them.

DELIVERY

THE REAL SPEECH IS NOT A PRACTICE SESSION

"When you are not practicing, remember, some-one somewhere is practicing...and when you meet him, he will win."

—Bill Bradley

To get better at speaking, you must practice. As Cicero stated, "The skill to do comes from the doing." Speaking is like any other skill—to improve, you must practice. If you want to become a better cook, you have to cook a lot. If you seek to improve your golf game, you have to play a lot of golf. So it is with speaking; you have to practice to get better. Bill Bradley, former basketball great and Senator from New Jersey, probably had basketball in mind when he made his remark about practice, but the statement applies equally well to speaking.

To improve and to succeed, practice is a requirement. The key to practicing presentations is to simulate the actual speaking situation as much as possible in your practice.

The first part of simulating your actual speaking situation is to practice aloud. It is easy to look over your notes and sound eloquent in your mind, but actually speaking the words adds a whole new element. The brain fills in gaps and awkward pauses when you just think about what you will say, but speaking the presentation aloud puts you on the spot just like an actual presentation. The first time you give your speech aloud is a practice session. If you don't practice aloud in advance, your presentation becomes a practice session. And like any practice session, it won't be as polished or professional as a finished product should be.

When you practice, use the notes you plan to use in the presentation. Don't type out neat, new notes that you haven't practiced with. You won't feel comfortable with them. If you plan to use a key word outline on note cards for the actual presentation, then practice with those cards. If you plan to use sheets of paper in acetate sleeves, then practice with those. By using your working notes for practice, you will learn where things are on the paper and become much more facile at working with the notes.

For your first practice run, you might just speak the presentation aloud at your desk or as you are driving. After the initial run-through, however, you need to also simulate the manner in which you will deliver the actual presentation. If possible, practice the speech aloud in the conference room, meeting room, or auditorium where the actual presentation will take place. If that isn't possible, just use an empty room, your office, or your basement. Stand and give your speech to an imaginary audience. Time yourself. Are you too long? Too short? How might you adjust the speech to better fit your time constraints? Note places where you stumbled, where you seemed unnatural or awkward, or where you had difficulty connecting a piece of support to a point. Should you eliminate it? Can you work out a phrasing that will work better? Consider your gestures. Did you incorporate purposeful movement? Is there a place that lends itself to a gesture to emphasize or illustrate? Only by practicing out loud and standing up will you become aware of these issues.

If your practice time is too long or too short, you need to edit your material. Some speakers mistakenly think they can expand on their ideas as they speak to adjust their time. In reality, if you need more length, try to think of other support for your points. If you need to cut something, however, the quickest and easiest way to cut is to eliminate an entire point. It is difficult to edit your own work. If you try to go through and remove tiny pieces of the presentation, you will agonize over the decisions and will only slowly reduce the presentation's length. If you take out a whole point, however, you make a significant impact without having to make a lot of decisions.

Many beneficial changes can be made when you practice alone, but an even closer simulation of the actual situation is to practice for a live audience—a coworker or a spouse, perhaps. Ask your mini-audience to listen to you and give you feedback. Better yet, videotape your practice session and critique yourself as you play it back. Have someone you respect critique the tape also. You will be amazed at how many things you will improve after watching yourself.

New speakers often ask, "How many times should I practice a presentation?" Practice until you feel comfortable with the material, but not so many times that you are tired of the content. Once you experience practice sessions, you will soon learn how much practice is enough. As a general guideline, though, you probably need to practice new material at least twice. If you practice five or six times, you are in danger of becoming too familiar with the material and making it sound flat, so the ideal is probably three to four practices.

Even if your presentation is one you have given several times before, practicing at least a section of it before you face a new audience still helps prepare you to be sharp. Any time you add new material to an old presentation, you need to practice that material until you feel comfortable with it. Look for any excuse to practice.

There isn't a better way to develop confidence and skill in your presentation than to practice. It takes time and is often arduous, thankless work, but the rewards are great. Practice is not time wasted, but time invested.

NOTEWORTHY

———⊷•⊶———

To use notes or not to use notes is a frequent question. Then if you do use notes, should you use cards, sheets of paper, or a script? Everyone has at one time or another listened to a speaker who read directly from notes or who had no idea how to use notes. That unfortunate speaker probably spent part of the time in delivering the speech either trying to find the notes or conceal them. The end result was a speaker who didn't seem very prepared when in reality using notes properly would have produced a very effective presentation.

Here we provide tips on the use of notes. If you follow them, you will look confident and demonstrate poise by using notes to enhance your message and take pressure away from you as you deliver your message.

Whatever system you use for notes, certain principles apply to all. Don't write out sentences, but use only key words or trigger words or phrases; the note should trigger your next thought. If it doesn't, then it's not a good note. Disciplining yourself not to include sentences or paragraphs as notes will enable you to think better on your feet and adapt more specifically to your audience. In addition, use lots of space for your notes. Don't scrunch up words to get more on a sheet of paper or notecard. You want the words easy to see and find once you look at your note. Finally, make sure your note is legible. If you can't read it when you look at it, you're in trouble.

You can handle notes in a variety of ways. First, you can use a notecard. Usually a 5 X 8 card is best—not so large that it looks like a cue card and not so small that it looks like a deck of cards. The notecard is easy to handle, and you are unlikely to lose it. You can hold it easily in your hand and make it an extension of your delivery style. Whatever you do, don't try to hide the card. Audience members know you are using notes, and hiding your notes only calls attention to them.

Keep the number of cards you use to a minimum. More than four cards are hard to keep track of. If you can't get your notes on four cards or fewer, you might want to consider the use of 8 $1/2$ X 11 sheets of paper protected by acetate sheets. The acetate covers not only protect your pages of notes but give them stability and make you look very professional with the dark piece of construction paper as the background the audience sees. This approach allows you to handle the pages like notecards and yet put more information on the page. These can be kept in a 3-ring binder when not in use or simply placed on the lectern to be picked up when needed. You might put these pages on the lectern and only refer to them when you are quoting directly. Looking at the page to read a quotation also gives you an opportunity to see if you have left out any critical piece of information. Again, making the page or pages an extension of your delivery gives you a natural, almost conversational manner that puts the audience at ease.

A third way of using notes is to let your visuals become your working outline as you speak. With a laptop presentation, slides, transparencies, or flip charts, you can create visuals that allow you to speak from what is on the screen instead of carrying notes with you. Be careful that you don't allow your eye contact to be towards the screen instead of with your audience.

One other alternative is on rare occasions when you must use a manuscript. Don't use a manuscript under most circumstances because it's too easy to simply read the speech to the audience. When you read your speech, you lose the spontaneity so important while speaking. The manuscript also makes it difficult to make eye contact with the audience and sounds dull and boring because you are reading.

But if you are speaking at a significant event where every word you speak is critical and must not be misquoted or taken out of context or is too technical just to use notes, keep these points in mind as you develop your manuscript. Type and double space with at least 14 point size. Type only two-thirds of the way down the page so that the audience won't just see the top of your head by the time you read down to the end of the page. End the page at the end of a paragraph so that there is a natural break to look up as you turn the page. Put in visual symbols in the margin to remind you to smile, make eye contact, punch out a key word, slow down, or speed up. Some of the symbols that we draw in our margins are:

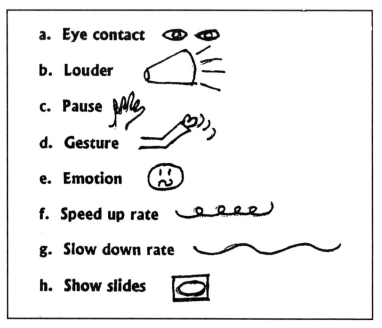

a. Eye contact

b. Louder

c. Pause

d. Gesture

e. Emotion

f. Speed up rate

g. Slow down rate

h. Show slides

Make sure these are visual symbols and not words because words may confuse you with the script. You do not want to read as part of content a note written to remind you to look up or speak louder!

Finally, don't use notes if you don't have to. Notes add another dimension to your presentation. If you do use notes, don't try to hide them; instead incorporate them into your delivery. Make the notes legible. Perhaps even color code your notes so that one color is used for main points and another color is used for subpoints; another color might be used just for statistics or quotations you read to your audience.

If you use them well, notes give you a sense of security if you forget in the middle of your presentation. Even if you never actually look at your notes, if you have them close by, you feel more confident about remembering what you want to say in your speech.

THE ART OF
SOUNDING SPOKEN

---◦•◦---

"A speech is not an essay on its hind legs."
—W. Norwood Brigance

We often write out our speeches as though they were essays, and we aren't successful in communicating to the audience. Some speakers put us to sleep primarily because the content of the speech is for the eye, not the ear. Words we speak are different from the words we write for a report. To be effective in front of an audience, you must prepare for the ear, not the eye. Here are some suggestions on how to do this.

First, think ideas, not words, as you prepare your speech. If you write the speech word for word, your speech will sound written, not spoken, and you may also be tempted to memorize the presentation. Preparing the speech by concentrating on ideas and not words will encourage you to be more spontaneous as you speak.

Second, use shorter sentences when you speak than when you write. This is easier on the ears and gives you more opportunity to pause and add emphasis to key words and thoughts. Short sentences give you more control over the nonverbal parts of the presentation. As speaker Earl Nightingale stated, "Keep your sentences short in a speech so you can breathe in the right places." Short sentences are a natural response to thinking ideas, not words, as you seek to speak a speech rather than read a script. Closely related to short sentences are short words. Keep things simple. Mark Twain once told of a Missouri farmer who ran five times for the state legislature without winning. It wasn't because he didn't practice his speeches. He practiced his campaign talks every day while milking. He referred to himself as "your humble aspirant." He referred to his audiences as "my enlightened constituents." He talked of "obtaining a mandate" for his "legislative mission." Then one day even his cow balked at his speeches and kicked him in the teeth. With his front teeth knocked out, the farmer could speak only words of one syllable. The result was he won his next election and kept getting reelected.

Third, don't be afraid to use contractions. "I can't understand the policy" is more direct and personal than, "I cannot understand the policy." Contractions give the speaker more opportunity for directness, a personal trait that is appealing to the listener. "Let's implement the system" is more direct and powerful than, "Let us implement the system."

Fourth, repetition anchors the ideas in the minds of the listener. As an audience, we only have one chance to get the ideas you speak. Repeat your ideas to help your audience remember. Use internal summary, for example. "Now that we have discussed contractions, let us move on to repetition." Preview your main ideas. Summarize them at the end as well. Repeat key points. Don't think of repetition as unnecessary redundancy; think of repetition, as political consultant James Humes calls it, as "echo words." These reinforce and remind audience members of what you've said. Franklin Roosevelt in his 1933 inaugural said, "The only thing we have to fear is fear itself." John F. Kennedy in his inaugural said, "Let us never negotiate out of fear but let us never fear to negotiate." Probably one of the most positive sentences to a listener may be, "Let me say that again...." The listener is happy because he or she was probably thinking, "I wish she would say that again." When you use any of the devices just listed for repetition, the listener is probably thanking you for it mentally.

Fifth, make your speech instantly clear. Use language the audience will understand. Your audience does not have a dictionary to find meanings as you speak. Immediately after speaking an idea, support it with an example or illustration. Illustration literally means to "make bright." An illustration will make your idea bright and stand out. For example, a recent newspaper article stated that it's dangerous to drive while using a cellular phone. A driver is four times as likely to have an accident while using a car phone. Doctors at Sunnybrook Health Science Centre in North York, Ontario, said driving while using a car phone is like driving with a blood-alcohol level at the legal limit. Comparisons are a speaker's best friend because they add instant clarity. Language can be instantly clear with the right definition. "We should look for serendipity. That is to say we should look for happy coincidences."

Sixth, use verbs that are vivid and conjure up a specific mental image to the listener. Try to use action verbs to do this. For example, the verb "walked" is concrete, but one might find a more specific way of portraying a person walking. A two-year-old "toddles" across the room, a drunk "staggers," and a conceited person "struts." Each of these is a specific variation of "walk." Also consider the verb "eat." A person not hungry may "pick" at food; a person really hungry may "wolf" down the food or "gulp" it down. Each is a variation that gives a more specific word picture to the listener.

Seventh, avoid cliches. A cliche is a statement, phrase, or word made trite by overuse. You lapse into cliches because your speaking vocabulary is not as extensive as your writing vocabulary, or because you haven't thought through carefully the idea you want to communicate, or because you're simply lazy with your speech habits. Eliminate worn-out phrases. If you have to say "in other words," you are admitting your first choice of words didn't work. Speak clearly the first time.

Eighth, eliminate filler words or sentences. Filler words are words that have no referent and don't give meaning to the listener. For many of us, filler phrases we sprinkle through our speeches are "you know" or "like." One language authority said facetiously that the introduction of "you know" in our speech reflects our hope that somebody somewhere knows what is going on. Eliminate filler words by simply pausing when you don't have something to say to give yourself some time to think or ponder or stress a point.

If you can be appealing to the ear, you can often avoid the problem of closed eyes and minds. Develop in your speech an oral quality to help ensure close attention and positive response to your message.

What Do I Do
With My Hands?

"A gesture does not exist alone in time."

—Martha Graham

In coaching individuals who are developing their presentation skills, one of the most frequent questions is, "What do I do with my hands?" Much nonverbal communication involves the use of hands. Your hands give specific messages to your audience; they tell the audience a great deal. You can show excitement or nervousness by the way you handle your hands. You can paint pictures or dramatize an event with your hands.

Sometimes your hands send messages you don't want your audience to receive. If you put them in your pockets, your audience believes you do not care about your topic; if you hold on to the lectern tightly with your hands, the audience might think you're nervous. If you fold your hands and arms together, the audience might think you don't care about them. So what do you do?

One way to make yourself get your hands involved early is to use a visual aid. To use a visual, you have to move! But there are less artificial ways to use your hands. Say, "I'm going to give you three reasons...." and hold up three fingers. Ask for a show of hands from your audience in response to a question and raise your own hand to illustrate the response you want. Tell a personal experience that allows you to point to yourself! If you use your hands early, you're more likely to use them later as well.

Only two reasons exist to use your hands in a speech: to illustrate and to emphasize. If you're not doing one of these two things, your use of hands is inappropriate. Scratching your nose, pulling on your ear, tapping the top of the lectern with your hands, and putting your hands in your pockets neither illustrate nor emphasize what you're saying—don't do these things.

For example, when you use your hands to tell about the size of the fish that got away or the depth of water in your basement after the last storm, you are illustrating to your audience. If you point to your audience as you stress what you want them to do as a result of your ideas, you are emphasizing the content of your speech.

To help yourself use your hands appropriately, have them in the "ready" position at the very beginning of your speech. You remember the old western movies where at some point the villain would be on Main Street causing trouble, and the sheriff or marshal would confront him. The camera would show the hands as each sought to draw first to shoot. The hands would be in the ready position first, hovering above the holster. Well, the speaker certainly isn't going to shoot the audience, but keeping hands in the "ready" position commits the speaker to use the hands and not hide them in pockets or grip or drum the lectern.

What you do with your hands in the opening minutes of your talk usually indicates whether they will be assets or liabilities as you speak. If you don't use your hands in your opening, you are less likely to use them later. It's important to use your hands to help communicate your ideas in the opening seconds of your speech.

Here are some general observations for using hands effectively as you speak. Keep them away from your face and below the neck level when you gesture. Hands around your face distract from meaningful facial expression and create a "busyness" around the head area. Don't take anything to the lectern with you besides your notes or pointer. Pens, paper clips, and chalk tempt you to play with them and create distractions. Have a specific place in the opening minute of your speech that absolutely requires the use of your hands to complete the thought. Don't bring your hands together; keep them apart. Too many distracting things occur (e.g., clasping, wringing, cracking knuckles) when you put your hands together. And when you're not making a gesture, just leave your hands in the "ready" position. It might feel awkward or unnatural to you, but it looks normal.

Remember that it's natural for you to use your hands as you speak. If you do not, you show a lack of poise and self confidence. It's very difficult to use the hands too much as long as your gestures have purpose.

ENERGY!
ENTHUSIASM!

"If you aren't fired with enthusiasm, you will be fired with enthusiasm."

—Vince Lombardi

Often how you say something is more important than what you say. In persuading or even helping people understand a concept or idea, you must demonstrate energy and enthusiasm about your topic. If you say, "I'm excited to talk to you about the importance of communication in your life," and yet say the statement without showing any emotion or energy, the audience isn't going to be responsive. How can you always appear energetic and enthusiastic in front of an audience?

Certain traits in a speaker seem to demonstrate energy and enthusiasm. First is movement. Just standing before an audience with hands grasping a lectern looks dull and boring. As the speaker, you need to move as you speak. Cheerleaders for a sports team show their excitement largely through movement. Certainly as speakers you don't want to jump up and down and raise your arms high in the air, but you can still learn from cheerleaders to use purposeful movement to demonstrate your excitement. Even a simple gesture toward your audience or a gesture back to you as you include yourself in the narrative shows energy and excitement. Movements with hands and arms are going to be easier as you choose not to hold on to the lectern, lean against a table, or hold on to sheets of notes. Avoiding holding on to things and keeping your hands out of your pockets will make it easier to enhance your content with movement.

Another simple technique is to move a step into your audience to show emphasis of a particular point. Beginning a new point, starting a story, or using a transition from one major section of your speech to another all present good opportunities to take that step.

To see how energy and enthusiasm play a significant role in the effectiveness of presentations, look at some of the popular television preachers. Turn the sound off first and just watch their movements. Their facial expressions are distinct and vivid. Gestures are large and sweeping. Each gesture seems to add to the point being made. Most preachers move freely without depending on a lectern and do so without losing contact with the audience.

Then turn the sound back on. Note how the quality now seems in synch with the movements. To underscore a scripture, the speaker will often pause before beginning to read and then punch out key words which reinforce a point being made. Listen as the preacher speeds up his or her rate and then slows down deliberately, putting emphasis on a key word. For the television evangelist, the visual connected with the sound is often what gives that speaker impact with the audience. To see such a combination, watch Jonas Nightengale, the traveling tent evangelist played by Steve Martin, in *Leap of Faith*. Early in the movie he delivers a tent meeting sermon. His assistant, played by Debra Winger, is communicating to him by an earplug radio. He begins his sermon, and the crowd seems dull and lethargic. So she tells him over the radio to do something to wake them up. The organ plays faster and louder. Martin incorporates quicker movements, speeds up his rate, and speaks louder and with bigger gestures. Immediately the crowd reacts in kind. Just changing his level of excitement and enthusiasm immediately affects the audience response to his message.

Visual aids add energy. Just referring to the screen as you talk about the visual or turning on the machine or laptop are appropriate movements. In smaller audiences where a flip chart is appropriate, tearing sheets off the tripod or flipping the sheet over the back of the tripod adds energy to your overall presentation.

As you paint pictures with words, seek to visualize with your hands and face how the picture looks or indicate size in how you describe the scene. You can show how long or how narrow a road is by hand and arm movements. You can demonstrate how dramatic an event is or how humorous a situation is by your facial expression. As you consider description or narrative in your speech, give consideration to how you make the picture more vivid and interesting by how you incorporate movements.

Look for one or two places in your speech where you can dramatically change the pace of your delivery by using movement. Perhaps at one point you show how long a pass was by exaggerating an arm throwing the ball, or you dramatize an explosion by throwing your arms high in the air. At the same time, use your voice to project even more feeling into what you are communicating to your audience. That moves us to the other part of showing energy and enthusiasm, which is the way you project with your voice.

A speaker must punch out words and phrases to show feeling and emotion. Excitement is partly determined by loudness for concern and softness for feeling. Even the pause before a key word or phrase can energize an audience. With the voice, always punch out key statistics with more volume. In speaking any proper noun, say it with added force. Just these two simple reminders will make you develop more feeling overall in your material.

The other area of emphasis is with the pause. Usually when you pause, you will punch out the next word as well as give emphasis to what has just been said. Pausing at the ends of sentences also helps you articulate your words more distinctly and allows the audience to follow you more easily.

To use the voice to show energy and enthusiasm, you must remember certain basic principles. To get the power to speak loudly and with feeling, you must draw power from the lower part of the chest area when you inhale. Like a set of bellows, the wider you open the bellows, the more force you have to blow on the fire. In like manner, the lower down in the diaphragm you can draw force for your voice, the louder your voice will be and the less strain you place on your vocal folds in the process. If you use only air from the upper chest area, you won't draw as much force and will put more strain on your vocal folds as you speak.

It's important to show energy and excitement in the way you use your voice, hands, arms, and facial expressions. One last point, which is also stressed elsewhere, is always to include material you feel very strongly about. Audiences can tell by your manner if you really believe strongly in your message. You can build in a certain amount of energy and enthusiasm just by presenting material that matters to you. Never include any idea, support, statistic, or story unless you firmly believe it adds to your overall theme and has power to make your ideas clearer. It's just easier to lose yourself in your material if you really like what you are talking about. Nervousness is lessened and confidence is increased when you have just the right material for you.

Remember, whatever you demonstrate in feeling or lack of it is going to affect your audience. Whatever you have is contagious! If you look out at the audience members and they look bored or disinterested, they are probably mirroring how you come across to them. So if your audience doesn't seem enthused about your topic as you speak, incorporate one of the suggestions mentioned above to get them back with you. Whatever you do, don't allow your audience to be bored without making an effort to draw them in with your enthusiasm and energy.

SEE WHAT I MEAN?

Transparencies, posters, models, pictures, or demonstrations can be great aids to the speaker. Visual aids can help the audience remember the point better. Visual aids attract the attention of the audience and help make your point more quickly and powerfully. The speaker shouldn't, however, use a visual aid just for the sake of using a visual aid; any time you use a visual, it requires more effort, and you must handle the visual aid even as you continue to speak. But because of what the visual aid can add to your presentation, consider the use of visuals in any speaking situation.

Here are some general criteria for visuals no matter what form the visual aid takes.

First, make sure the visual is large enough for everyone to see. If you can't make it large enough, then don't use it.

Always check it out first. Put the visual where you plan to use it and then sit in the chair farthest away from the visual to determine if it can be seen.

Second, conceal the visual before and after you use it. People are curious and will stare at it when you aren't using it. Once you have illustrated your point with the visual, put it away so that people won't keep thinking about it after you have moved on to another point.

Third, be comfortable using it. Practice showing the visual aid so that it becomes an extension of you as you speak. The more familiar you are handling the visual, the more confident you will appear as you speak. Familiarity also reduces the chances of something going wrong.

Fourth, if the visual involves something mechanical, be sure to check out the equipment before the presentation starts. Anticipate anything that might go wrong and have a contingency plan ready. Be sure you have extra markers, an extra bulb, or extra outlets for electrical equipment.

Fifth, don't let your body hinder people from seeing the visual. Step to the side of the screen and don't block the view. Speak to the audience, not to the visual aid. Hold the visual at the eye level of the audience and in front of you.

Finally, don't allow the visual to become a silent demonstration. As you use the visual, keep the flow of speech going. Remember your visual is an aid to you, so don't allow it to become the main event. You are still in control.

Let's look now at specific types of visual aids and how to use them.

One of the most common and versatile types is the overhead projector. This can be used with most sizes of audiences and with no light or a room full of light. The speaker has full control of the visual with just the flip of the switch. You can easily grab the attention of the audience by turning the machine on or off. With the easy access to copying machines for transparencies, the speaker can easily magnify or reduce a visual for easy use with the overhead. The transparencies can fit easily into a briefcase for simple transportation. Another benefit is if you use the cardboard frame, you can put your notes on Post-Its and place them on the frame. In fact, the transparency can substitute for your set of notes. Disadvantages of the overhead are you must have access to the machine, which can be troublesome to carry around, and you must be prepared to deal with mechanical problems. Don't depend on the overhead for your complete presentation in case something goes wrong.

A second type of visual is the flip chart. It is used primarily for small groups and can usually be used for up to 40 people. As you speak, you can write on it easily, and the flip chart gives you an intimacy with the group because of its spontaneity. You have ample flexibility with different color markers and the ability to draw, write, or print. The flip chart is a great way to underscore the value of a particular statistic or the meaning of a specific word. This visual also gives a flare for the dramatic as you turn the page back. Suspense is easily added with the use of the flip chart. Be sure to make the print large enough. A good rule to follow is no more than six lines on the sheet and no more than six words on a line—remember it as the 6 by 6 rule. Because flip charts typically have flimsy pages, if you prepare the flip chart before the presentation begins, have a cover page so that people aren't exposed to the flip chart before you are ready for them to see the material. When you have audience participation and you want to record people's comments, the flip chart is an excellent vehicle. Tape the various sheets on the walls as you complete them, and your visuals can be as up to date as the last comment from an audience member.

A third type of visual aid is the slide projector. It can be used for more formal presentations and with large audiences. The slides can enhance your credibility because they look professional and make you appear more so. A remote control is essential, and you should get comfortable using the slide projector with practice. It is critical to check out each slide before you use it in a presentation. Seeing slides in the small frame is much different from seeing them on the screen. Another disadvantage of using the slide projector is you have to dim the lights to see the slide easily. This may affect the attention level of audience members, and it's harder for you to see the audience. Again, don't depend too heavily on this visual aid; because a slide projector has more moving parts, more can go wrong.

Another type of visual is the poster. A poster can be prepared ahead of time and can add vividness and impact. Posters are cumbersome to handle, and the same information can easily be put on a transparency or slide. But the poster is a good change of pace and might be easier to handle if you only use one or two instead of the more complicated machinery of the slide or even overhead projector.

The model is a good change of pace for the audience and is often combined with a demonstration. You can take it apart, or put it together, or show how something works. Remember to keep talking as you show or demonstrate with it. People are usually curious about models, so be careful to conceal it before and after use.

Pointers are effective ways of highlighting specific parts of the visual. Laser pointers are marvelous because they can be seen in full lighted rooms and a long distance from the screen. Even the simple periscope pointer can be useful to keep the speaker from getting in front of the visual and hiding part of it.

Your speech might have dynamite content and clear structure, but it could still benefit from a visual aid. Be creative—a memorable visual not only keeps people's attention at the time, it helps them remember your entire speech! For example, our friend, trainer Dave Bryant, told of an associate who gave speeches on concrete, and audiences were going to sleep as he spoke. It was a technical subject with lots of data. Dave told him he needed a "concrete example." So he began taking with him to his speeches a disc of concrete to show as he spoke. The speaker said the change was dramatic. People stayed awake during his speeches on concrete.

Ensure success in your next speech. Use a visual aid!

HANDLING VISUALS
MADE FROM
PRESENTATION SOFTWARE

O verhead projectors and flip charts are being replaced with a variety of presentation software such as PowerPoint, Charisma, Freelance Graphics, and Astound. These tools may seem awkward at first, but here are suggestions to make the transition easier.

First, keep your slides simple. With all the "bells and whistles" available on software packages, a temptation to include every possible variation on each slide exists. Use an uncluttered template. Keep the color combination simple and complementary. The six by six rule applies here as well.

Second, label points on each slide for maximum impact. It is best to use bullets instead of numbering each point. Numbering each point tends to imply that some points are more important than others; bullets indicate equality. In addition, you may forget which number you are on as you speak. Current software offers you more bullet choices than you can imagine.

Be consistent in your style and use of bullets. Use the same bullet shape for all points at the same level of importance. Keep the lines of your text parallel in construction. For example, begin each line with a noun or verb, but not a mixture of both. In addition, bulleted items look best when aligned on the left margin of the slide instead of being centered.

Third, make the point size of a font easy to read and follow on a slide. A font is a collection of letter shapes and numbers in one size, weight, and style. The point size of a font refers to the size of the letters. Most presentation text should be a minimum of 24 points. Titles should be 36 points or larger. Don't make the point size too large, or it will seem like the slide is shouting at the audience.

Color is easy to develop on presentation software. Learn to use it to your advantage. Blue makes a good background color; black does not. Readability is critical, so choose highly contrasting colors. For example, use white or yellow against dark blue backgrounds. Warm colors such as yellow are brighter and more dynamic than cool colors such as green or blue. Warm colors present action, for example, and cool colors indicate status or efficiency. Be careful about red. Although it can promote action or stimulate the audience, red also reminds people of corrections and mistakes.

Be consistent with the colors of your slides throughout the presentation, and again, keep them simple. Change colors only for emphasis or contrast. Too many colors are a distraction to the eye and the mind. Remember that unusual colors may be distracting to audience members.

Remember that the computer software does not take your place as speaker. Make sure that the slides are subordinate to you the speaker. For example, stand facing the audience looking at the laptop screen which is set up in front of you. This allows you to look at the audience even as you glance at the computer screen. Use a remote mouse to give you freedom to move around. Stand to the left of the screen which makes it easier on your audience to look from the speaker to the screen and then read the visuals from left to right. Have a printed set of slides nearby with your notes so that you know what is coming next on the screen. Anticipate the time you have programmed between slides or the time it will take to move from one slide to another if you are making the changes manually. Pictures, clip art, charts, and video clips add variety to a presentation. Be sure that your computer can support the type of presentation you are making. Ask yourself the following questions as you prepare your software presentation.

1. Is the picture or clip art necessary to make the point?

2. Is there anything in the picture or clip art that would offend?

3. Will the colors look the same in the presentation as they do on my laptop in my office?

4. Are the numbers on the charts rounded off as much as possible so that people can quickly understand them?

5. Is the video clip short enough that my audience will not have a hard time giving their attention back to me quickly?

6. Does the picture, chart, or clip art look too busy?

When using charts, keep in mind that line charts are best to show trends, bar charts are best to show comparisons, and pie charts are best at showing proportions.

To move from the faithful overhead projector to presentation software, equipment, as well as style, must change. You will need a laptop with presentation software loaded on it, a projection unit, and a screen. A table next to the projection system is needed for you to set your computer on. You will probably also need an outlet strip and extension cord to accommodate the projection system and laptop. Last, you will need a pointer and a remote mouse.

Beware that you are entering an entirely different price range when you move into presentation software. A projection unit will cost several thousand dollars, and you will need a powerful laptop or PC. Although the new generation of projectors produces much brighter light, you will still need to dim the lights in order for people to see all of your slides clearly. Always have a backup system with the overhead projector and transparancies ready to go. You never know when the presentation software will malfunction, and it is difficult to remedy while a live audience is watching you work.

Finally, remember the presentation software will make it more challenging for you to have the active delivery style that you are comfortable with in using flip charts or the overhead. Even with the remote mouse, you have more to think about in keeping track of where you are with the slides, and as a result you are less comfortable at first in moving away from your laptop and screen.

Used well, presentation software makes you look more professional and in control as you address the audience.

THE POWER
OF PRESENCE

———•◦•———

S ome speakers stand to begin their presentations and
immediately command the attention and respect of
their audiences. Ronald Reagan, Lee Iacocca, Eliza-
beth Dole, Martin Luther King, Jr.—all of these effective
speakers seemed to have a quality that made people want to
listen. In school you might have noticed a difference among
your teachers or professors as well; some were well-organized and used a variety of teaching techniques, but you
were bored in their classes. Others, however, did many of
the same things but made you excited about their classes.
Why the difference? Speakers who have immediate impact
possess the quality of presence. Presence makes the audience feel at ease and willing to listen. It exudes speakers'
calm confidence that they control their situations. Fortu-

nately, though some speakers seem endowed with an extra portion of presence, anyone can develop greater presence and, consequently, greater presentation power.

First, think of public speaking as simply enlarged conversation. A speaker seeks to connect with the audience in a personal way even though there might be 500 people in that audience. In speaking to a group, you converse the same way you do in one-on-one conversation, except that you adjust to the size of the group. In conversing with another person, for instance, it's natural to gesture and use different facial expressions. In fact, it would be very strange to watch someone talk who never moved or showed any change in facial expression. Yet when faced with a public speaking situation, many people become almost robotic. Every movement seems forced and mechanical—if there is any movement at all. Faces are frozen, and tone of voice never changes. Keep your conversational style when speaking publicly. Just adapt so that fifty people can hear you instead of five.

Second, use your unique style when you speak. Don't try to imitate another speaker in delivery or content. Many observers criticized Bill Clinton's 1997 Inaugural Address because in spite of its good ideas, many of those ideas seemed borrowed from past inaugural addresses. Someone who sounds *like* someone else will never measure up to the real thing, so you might as well use your own style. In displaying your own unique style, avoid mechanical gestures and word choices that don't fit the way you communicate best and most comfortably. Your speaking vocabulary and body movement shouldn't differ significantly from your conversational vocabulary and body movement, except that your movements need to be visible to a larger audience.

How else can you include your personality and uniqueness as you speak in order to develop presence? A Dairy Queen employee showed an example of this a few years ago in Cherokee, North Carolina. If you've ever had a Blizzard from Dairy Queen, you know that it's a really thick ice cream concoction. Steve likes his with crushed Butterfinger candy bars in it. After the young Dairy Queen employee in Cherokee took the order, he mixed the Blizzard, and suddenly turned the Blizzard upside down and then right side up all in the same motion with a pizzazz Steve had never before witnessed. He demonstrated that this really was the thickest possible Blizzard Steve could hope for! His action and flair made Steve want that Blizzard even more. The employee could have half-heartedly gone through the motions of his demonstration, or he could have even said, "This is a thick Blizzard." But he showed a uniqueness with his nonverbals that is remembered these years later. How can you demonstrate your uniqueness as you address an audience? What separates you from other speakers? The answer might be a technique for developing presence. One speaker has a variety of unusual-looking glasses. Use your unique traits to establish presence as well.

Third, maintain good posture. Some speakers look awkward and not in control because of their posture; their feet are not a good distance apart, or they shift their weight from foot to foot and create a lot of unnecessary and distracting movement. Some speakers stand like storks, with all of their weight on one foot. Occasionally, they shift all of their weight to the other foot. Over time, this creates an effect like the pendulum on a clock! Some speakers act like expectant fathers, pacing and shifting their feet to burn off nervous energy without any real purpose. Some speakers slouch and make themselves look small. To build presence with your posture, balance the weight of your body equally on the balls of your feet as you start to speak. This will give you optimum height and a steady, confident demeanor as you stand before the group. With your weight on the balls of your feet, it will also be very difficult for you to move without making a conscious decision to do so. This helps eliminate swaying and shifting, which makes you look uncertain and takes away from your presence.

Keeping your posture open also invites the confidence and attention of your audience. Gesture toward audience members instead of away from them. Keep your gestures below your face so that people can see your facial expressions. Don't cross your arms and thus isolate yourself from the audience. With a large audience, gesture from the shoulder out, and with a small audience or with low ceilings, gesture from the elbow out. Gestures of those sizes will be appropriate for those audiences.

Fourth, keep your hands in the "ready" position discussed in the chapter on what to do with your hands. Speakers who never seem to find a place for their hands as they speak, or speakers who attach their hands and arms to the lectern as if it alone is tethering them to earth don't generate presence that moves the audience. Some speakers rub their hands together, repeatedly clasp and unclasp their hands, or continually put their hands in and out of their pockets, putting their audiences on edge. With your hands at your sides, you look natural, and your hands are ready to quickly come up to make a purposeful gesture.

Another key to presence is maintaining a pleasant expression. Smile before you start to speak and continue to look pleasant as you develop your ideas. Look out at your audience as you start. You can do this because you have learned your introduction better than any other part of your presentation. To make eye contact, mentally divide your audience into four or five relatively equal "clumps." This technique works whether you speak to four people or four hundred. Move your gaze from clump to clump, and everyone will feel a personal contact with you. Avoid looking down at the floor, up at the ceiling, or just slightly above people's heads. Despite what you might have heard, if you look just above people's heads, it looks like you are actually looking just above people's heads. You won't fool anyone, and you certainly won't demonstrate presence. You'll simply look as though you are avoiding eye contact.

Finally in being a speaker with presence, do or say something in the opening minutes that shows your listeners you have prepared this speech specifically for them. You might use a term unique to your audience, or you might mention an experience group members have all shared. If you demonstrate that the content of your speech is focused on the specific needs of your audience, members will respect you and want to hear more.

These simple ideas will help you become a speaker with presence. That presence will be a powerful tool in making you more memorable, your audience more attentive, and your message more persuasive.

POISE AND PROFESSIONALISM

HANDLING
THE BUTTERFLIES

———◆———

"When I'm nervous, I'm comfortable; when I'm
not nervous, I'm uncomfortable"

> —Michael Johnson,
> 1996 Olympic gold medalist
> in the 200 and 400 meters,
> on nerves before a race

"Luck is when preparation meets opportunity."

> —Elmer Letterman

Almost everyone who has ever had to speak has experienced stagefright. This feeling of nervousness goes by different names—you might call it speech apprehension, communication apprehension, excessive anxiety, or even having butterflies in your stomach. Whatever you call it, some very real physical symptoms exist.

Stagefright includes involuntary movements of the hands and knees when speaking. A person with stagefright might feel nausea or an urge to go to the bathroom. People with stagefright can have quavering voices and can suddenly forget what comes next in the presentation. Stagefright can make you want a glass of water (or something stronger!). It can give you a dry throat, a rapid heartbeat, cold and clammy hands, or lots of perspiration. Over the years, our students have experienced all kinds of stagefright problems. In the middle of his speech, one student simply said, "I don't feel very well"—and then passed out on the floor. Another student lost his voice while speaking. He would start out with normal projection, but by the end of the five-minute presentation, he had only a whisper. Another student had enough volume, but could only speak haltingly, as if English were not his native language.

These are obviously examples of debilitating stagefright, but the nervousness of stagefright is not necessarily a bad thing—in moderation. In fact, a little nervousness usually makes your thinking clear and helps you feel energized. The key, then, isn't to eliminate stagefright, but to control it. As Edward R. Murrow said, "Stagefright is the sweat of perfection. The only difference between the pros and the novices is that the pros have trained the butterflies to fly in formation."

Here are some tips on how to handle the butterflies.

First, prepare. No substitute exists for careful preparation. When you haven't planned or practiced what you are going to say, then you deserve to be nervous. Carefully pondering your topic, developing an outline, and practicing will help you have confidence—and less nervousness—when it's your turn to speak.

Second, develop positive thoughts as your time to speak approaches. We often allow negative thoughts to overwhelm us. We think, "What am I doing here?" or "These people don't want to hear what I have to say." Such ideas do nothing but increase anxiety. Instead of these negative thoughts, repeat this script in your mind: "I'm ready for this presentation." "What I have to say will be helpful to these people." You cannot think both a negative and a positive thought at the same time, so this positive script will push aside negativity. A statement about selling applies equally well to speaking—"Your most important sale is to sell yourself to yourself." Positive thoughts build your confidence and decrease your nervousness.

Be careful how you treat your body before speaking. Not enough sleep can make you more nervous and irritable. Drinking too much caffeine or eating high sugar content food can heighten your anxiety level. Not eating at all can also create problems. You might feel weak and your stomach might make embarrassing noises. When people pass out from stagefright, lack of food is often a contributing factor.

Give yourself enough time so that you don't have to hurry to reach your speaking engagement on time. Rushing and worrying about traffic or speeding can lead to more anxiety. Not only do you want to plan carefully the content of your speech, you also want to plan carefully the circumstances leading to your getting to the site in a timely manner. Allowing plenty of extra time gives you a chance to handle any emergencies and have your speaking situation under as much control as possible. Recently, Steve got to his speaking room and found the room to be ninety degrees when it was thirty degrees outside. He was able to have the room cooled by the time his presentation began. But if he had gotten to the speech just on time, his nervousness—and speaking challenges—would have been increased dramatically by the unusually hot room.

Before you start to speak, another way to handle stagefright is to become acquainted with audience members you don't already know. Sit down at a table and introduce yourself. No longer are audience members strangers, but friends. Just the exercise of shaking hands and meeting people will take your mind off your nervousness and focus it on your audience, where it should be. In addition, the people you have met will probably smile at you when you begin to speak—you are building yourself a supportive audience.

Work hard on the opening material. If you get off to a good start, you relax quickly because you can see your audience is responding positively. On the other hand, if you stumble or have weak material in the beginning, audience members will show their lack of interest; their unfavorable reaction will increase your nervousness. You may have some of the longest minutes of your life as you seek to get off the platform. To get off to a good start, have a clever or thought-provoking opening. Use a quotation, or, if you feel comfortable using humor, begin with a funny line or anecdote. Put some of your strongest material in the opening minutes of your speech, and the positive feedback of the audience will build your confidence and help you control your butterflies.

Once you do begin speaking, focus on friendly faces. Some people in your audience will always have dour expressions on their faces, but you're not necessarily the cause of their displeasure. They might have had a fight at home, be suffering from indigestion, or just always wear unpleasant expressions. As speakers, though, we often fear that any negative expression is a reaction to something we have said or done. When you look over your audience, don't linger on these people. Instead, find friendly faces. They will always be present as well, and focusing on them will help increase your confidence that you are delivering a message people want to hear and that you are delivering it well.

Different people have different manifestations of stagefright, but we all have nervousness from time to time. In fact, be concerned if you feel no nervousness at all; you need some nervousness to keep your mind at its sharpest. Remember, everyone suffers from stagefright at one time or another. Take comfort in this and work on handling your butterflies so that even your Monarchs fly in formation.

MOLDING THE SPEECH

TO FIT YOUR AUDIENCE

---◆◆◆---

From the very beginning in developing your skills as a presenter, one of the keys to success is to pay attention to your audience. While it's easier to find a new audience than to find a new presentation, that doesn't mean you should deliver identical presentations to different audiences. Being successful as a presenter requires not only a well-developed argument that creatively makes a point, but also adaptation of the presentation to your specific audience. Even if your presentation is for a group within your organization, you need to find out as much as possible about the specific organization members who will compose your audience. Remember this: THE MORE YOU KNOW ABOUT YOUR AUDIENCE, THE MORE EFFECTIVE YOU WILL BE AS A PRESENTER.

Russell Conwell lived this principle. He delivered his speech, "Acres of Diamonds," over 6,000 times. With the more than eight million dollars he earned, he helped establish Temple University. How could he give the same presentation that many times? He prepared for each audience he spoke to. He didn't deliver the same presentation 6,000 times, he delivered 6,000 *adaptations* of the same presentation. Before a speaking engagement, Conwell would go into the city or community and talk to people who lived there. He would ask the movers and shakers in the community about their concerns, problems, and successes. Then he would relate the basic idea of his presentation, that opportunities abound right where we are, to specific situations in that community. Conwell was successful because he made each presentation audience-specific.

The more directed your material is to the specific audience, the more effective you will be in your presentation. Knowing what audience members hope to learn from your presentation helps you meet their expectations. Being aware of whether attendance was optional prepares you for the receptiveness level of the audience. A little bit of basic audience analysis can tremendously improve your ability to make your message have impact.

FIND ANSWERS TO THESE QUESTIONS ABOUT YOUR AUDIENCE:

1. What do audience members expect to get out of your presentation?

---

2. What do they already know about your presentation topic?

3. What will they do immediately before they come to your presentation?

4. What motivation do audience members have to accept the material in your presentation? Do you have information that will help them solve specific problems? Have they chosen to hear you, or were they required to?

5 What do people in the audience have the power to do based on your presentation?

6. Are there any buzz words, jargon, or issues that your audience will respond to in a very positive or a very negative way?

The answers to these questions help you prioritize which information to present. They also help you know what emphasis you need to place on entertainment as opposed to teaching. With an understanding of your audience members' knowledge levels and needs, you are well on your way to tailoring a presentation that will fit them. Basic demographic questions can also help prepare you for a specific audience. An older group, for example, has a better sense of history and can identify with more historical events than a younger audience can. Younger audiences have grown up on television and expect a fast-paced, fact-filled presentation—and usually demand entertainment as well.

USEFUL AUDIENCE DEMOGRAPHIC QUESTIONS

1. How many people will be in the audience?

2. What is the distribution between men and women?

3. What is the age range for the group?

4. How experienced in their fields are most audience members?

5. What are the typical job responsibilities for audience members?

6. Other than all being present for this speech, what other commonalities do audience members share?

How do you find the answers to these questions? Usually one person is willing to go to great lengths to get the information you need about an audience: your informant. The informant is the audience member most responsible for choosing you as a speaker (this is often the program planner). If you do well, that person looks good; if you do poorly, that person will bear the blame after you leave. Ask that person for any information you need because the informant is highly motivated to help you succeed.

Audience analysis is more than just answering a series of questions, however. Try to develop some understanding of the culture in which audience members work. If it's another section of your own organization, how is it different from what you are used to? If you are speaking at a convention or to a group with which you are unfamiliar, you can research many questions. Is it a union shop? Is it a *Fortune*

500 company or a mom and pop operation? Is it publicly traded or closely held? Does it primarily serve government or business? Is it service or manufacturing oriented? How long has it existed? To find answers to these questions, scan business sections of newspapers, read *The Wall Street Journal*, and secure copies of the organization's mission statement, annual report, or even recent speeches by leaders to employees or stockholders. Ask for copies of any in-house publication. In all of these resources, not only will you get a better idea of what the organization is about, but you will also learn about buzz words, hot topics, and any recent problems or successes that the group has experienced. You might even find anecdotal material for the content of your presentation.

Adaptation also includes finding out about the physical surroundings of your presentation. Will the presentation be in a company meeting room? Is it in an offsite hotel meeting room? Is it in a resort area where people are easily distracted by recreational activities? Is it in a well-lighted room? Does the room have windows? Is it in a large or small room? Is it on the twentieth or second floor? Are chairs movable or bolted to the floor? Is it in a theater? Auditorium? Classroom? Are the ceilings high or low? Is it a fully equipped media room or will equipment need to be moved in? Once you have learned about your location, you can either request the changes you need or decide how to cope with the way things are.

Learning about personalities of people in the audience helps your adaptation also. Ask your informant for the names and phone numbers of some specific people who will be in the audience, and seek their advice on how to be effective for this specific group. Recently, in talking to a person who would be in the audience, Steve learned that many had recently left the organization because of an early retirement incentive they couldn't resist. Thus, he would have a number of new employees in the audience. This information helped focus his preparation.

Get to the meeting room early to meet people. Learn some names. Find out what hobbies certain audience members have. You might even find someone who is the group's "class clown" and ask to mention the person in one of your jokes or stories. Personalize as much as possible as you prepare to speak. You will see some of the most supportive smiles at the beginning of your presentation from the people you met or talked to before the presentation began.

Even after you have performed all of this audience analysis, however, you must still put your newfound information to good use. You can build your credibility in several ways by illustrating to the audience that you have done your homework.

Mention the name of the specific group to which you are speaking in the first thirty seconds of your presentation. Refer to someone in the group by name in the opening minutes of your presentation. Use a story or example from the company or organization to which you are speaking. Use the company logo in one of your visuals (but be sure to obtain permission first). Refer to one of the products or services the organization produces or perhaps refer to another of the organization's locations. Incorporate a part of the mission statement into one of your points. Use stories you believe will appeal to the habits, age, and sex of audience members. All of these actions demonstrate your careful preparation and make audience members more willing to listen to you.

An important part of preparation is preparing for the specific audience. You might have excellent organization, relevant evidence for your points, an interesting introduction, and a dramatic conclusion. But if you haven't spent time preparing for your audience, you will still have a mediocre presentation. The more you know about your audience, the more effective your presentation will be.

THE SPEECH
TO AN AUDIENCE
FROM A DIFFERENT CULTURE

———•◦•———

S tartling fact: more people in the world speak English as a *second* language than those who speak English as a native language. Startling fact number two: some of them are coming soon to an audience near you! Some of these people immigrate to English-speaking countries. Others become part of organizations with global interests, meaning they might be transferred to an English-speaking country or at least do business in one. Other times, you might be required to travel to audience members outside your home country who don't speak English as their primary language. Because of the increase in cross-cultural speaking situations like these, you need to understand some simple strategies for making yourself understood and avoiding conflict when you are faced with audience members who don't speak English as a native tongue.

If a translator is not provided for your presentation, you can assume most of your audience members have at least a basic knowledge of English. But to ensure that they understand as much as possible, use short words. Think of your own foreign language experience—even many years after studying a language, the words you probably remember are the short ones. The same is true for people who have learned English as a second language. Almost anything can be said in one- or two-syllable words, and using shorter words increases the likelihood your audience will understand you.

As you speak, be careful to enunciate. Pronounce your words clearly and distinctly to avoid misunderstanding. For example, an American, Paul, one of Josh's fellow teachers in Ukraine, had a student who spoke excellent English. One day when she arrived to study with him, he asked, "Did you have a nice weekend?" She gave him a blank look and began leafing through her English-Russian dictionary. He thought she would understand each word he had said, so he asked, "What are you looking up?" She responded, "Didja!" If you run your words together and fail to enunciate properly, it sounds to the untrained ear as if you are using a completely different word.

Simply slowing down your rate helps you enunciate, and speaking more slowly is another key to making yourself understood. Again, if you have ever studied a foreign language, remember how much easier it is to understand when someone slows down; you have a little more time to think about each word. In certain parts of the United States, people have a special tendency to speak rapidly, and for all native speakers, slowing down at least a little bit will improve understanding. You shouldn't slow your rate so much that you insult the audience, but between baby talk and the speed at which you would speak to your best friend is a happy medium.

Avoid euphemisms. When your audience members are not perfectly fluent in English, your best bet is to be blunt instead of trying to make something sound better or more interesting. In the English language, for instance, we have dozens of ways to talk about "death" without ever using that word. But if you talk about someone "passing on" in a presentation, your audience might be left wondering, "To where?" We also have many ways of talking about good or poor performance. If you tell non-native English speakers that results "tapered off" or "went through the roof," you are likely to have at least some confused listeners. Be direct. Be blunt.

For particularly important information, repeat your idea using different words, especially if you sense from the audience's response that the meaning is not clear. This doubles the chance people will understand what you mean. To an audience of native speakers, this would sound redundant, but with a cross-cultural audience, it just makes good sense, as in, "We need an increased customer base. You must sell our product to more people." For example, Josh's friend Kevin, an American, was looking for a restroom in downtown Kiev, and the woman he was asking couldn't comprehend any word he could think of—"restroom," "bathroom," "toilet," even "water closet." Finally, out of exasperation, he asked, "Excrement?" and she gave him directions. Word something multiple ways, and your communication will improve.

In the content of your speech, guard against ethnocentrism, which is the attitude that your culture is the best culture and cultures that do things differently are inferior. If you use an ethnocentric tone in your presentation to people from somewhere else, you aren't likely to be very persuasive. So don't complain about having to drive on the "wrong" side of the road. Different countries sometimes have different time orientations, and it might exasperate you that to your way of thinking, people are always late; again, that might simply be the way things are done in, for instance, an island or South American culture. Avoid speculating about how much people from other cultures should love your country because of all the different things it has. If you are in a former Soviet country, refrain from telling jokes about Communists.

If you have a translator, share some of the main points of your presentation with that person before the presentation. Check to make sure the translator understands jargon or technical language you plan to use. And during your presentation, stop after each complete thought so that the translator can speak.

The next time your audience consists of people who understand other languages better than they understand English, don't panic. Communication is possible, but you must slow down and simplify.

ON SITE PREPARATION:

OR, PREPARATION
MEANS MORE THAN CONTENT

———•◦•◦•———

A critical part of preparation for your next presentation has nothing to do with what you actually plan to say. Information about your topic and your audience isn't the only knowledge you need to have when you stand to deliver your presentation. Here are some ideas about the additional preparation you must do to be effective in your next presentation.

First, know how long you have to speak. This is not only an ethical concern, but a practical concern. People in the audience know when they expect you to finish, and you need to know as well. But what if your informant tells you to take as much time as you need? Then ask, "How long do speakers usually speak?" The answer to this question will give you at least a general time frame to stay within. You might be thinking "around 30 minutes," while your audience might be expecting "about 15 minutes." Find out your stated or unstated time constraints as specifically as possible. Audience members get impatient if you go overtime even when your content is excellent. Quit on time or even a couple of minutes early.

Second, know the temperature of the room where you speak. As we mentioned before, get to the room early, check it out, and talk to people in charge if it's too hot. Audience members get lethargic and sleepy if the room is too warm. Coldness isn't as much of a concern; the body heat of the audience tends to warm up the room, and a cold room often makes people more alert and responsive. David Letterman's audiences always complain about how cold his studio is, but the coldness works to his advantage in getting laughs and participation from his audience.

Third, know how flexible the public address system is. Is the room so small that you don't need a microphone? If you need amplification, is the microphone stuck to the lectern? A stationary microphone binds you to a spot. If there is a stationary microphone, ask for a cordless microphone or a handheld one with enough cord for you to move away from the lectern. A wireless or handheld microphone gives you flexibility to be a more active speaker. If possible, hold the microphone in your hand or clip it to your clothing and test it before the audience arrives. It is particularly important to test a wireless microphone. If you use a wireless, check two things: that you know how to turn it on (there is often a "mute" setting) and that the battery is still good.

Fourth, know the primary expectation for your presentation. Do people expect you to motivate, entertain, or inform? Or do all three? If motivation is the key, then you don't have to be as concerned about imparting a lot of new information. If the main concern is information, include visuals or hand-outs that guarantee audience members "take away" material. If motivation and entertainment are your primary purposes, then you want to send people away with positive feelings, which will probably require humor and stories from you. The individual who will be most helpful with this presentation preparation is your informant, or the person who asked you to speak, because your informant has the most at stake in the success of your presentation. To best understand your presentation's purpose, ask, "What do you want to happen as a result of this presentation?"

Take time to check the headlines and key issues in the newspaper the day you speak. You never know when there could be a relevant example or statistic to make the main point of your presentation even more powerful. One speaker *always* includes in his presentation something from that day's newspaper—he feels like it makes all of his material seem more current. A recent article in the *Wall Street Journal* discussed the trend for job interviewers to ask applicants to give presentations on how they might handle hypothetical problems. This tidbit would have been powerful to include if that day or that week you were speaking on the value of developing speaking skills.

Remember, knowledge of subject is critical. Often, however, knowledge of elements beyond the content of your presentation will make the difference between a presentation that is fair and a presentation that is fantastic!

ETHICS:
MORE THAN HONESTY

"Few souls are saved after the first 20 minutes of a sermon."

—Mark Twain

A student began a persuasive speech by spreading garbage out on a table. She said, "What do all of these pieces of trash have in common? They can all be recycled." And she gave a good speech on the need for recycling and how to set up community recycling programs. She finished to a nice round of applause and then gathered up all of the recyclables from the table—and threw them away in the wastebasket in the corner. She obviously didn't understand the need for speakers to act in ways consistent with their messages in order to maintain credibility.

Developing and maintaining a reputation as an honest, trustworthy person is invaluable to the speaker. Being accepted as credible is a basis for any speech; without the foundation of audience trust, a speech will flop.

THE POWER OF A PRESENTATION TO ESTABLISH CREDIBILITY

The year was 1952, and Dwight Eisenhower was running for president with Richard Nixon as his vice-presidential candidate. Charges surfaced, however, that Nixon had illegally used some campaign contributions, and Eisenhower considered dropping Nixon from the ticket. In what became known as the "Checkers Speech," Nixon defended himself in a 30-minute, nationally televised speech. With his wife Pat sitting in the background, he defended his ethics, at one point holding up a piece of paper he claimed was the result of an audit of his books finding him blameless. Nixon did admit, however, that some supporters had given his children a dog. He said the kids had named the dog "Checkers," and no matter what anyone said, he wasn't going to let them take that dog away. He concluded by asking people to telegraph or mail to the Republican National Committee their opinion of whether or not he should continue to run with Eisenhower. The overwhelmingly positive response assured his

---

> place in the campaign. Who knows how much of American history for the next twenty years was changed because of a little dog and a presentation that convinced people of Richard M. Nixon's credibility.

In addition to the fundamental issue of honesty and credibility, a speaker must meet other ethical standards to maintain the trust and respect of audience members. Speakers might as well quit if their audiences don't respect them and what they have to say.

Although preparation has been discussed in other chapters, good preparation is an ethical requirement as well as a practical one. Your audience has given you time and an opportunity, and audience members deserve to hear your best effort. That only comes through careful preparation. If they can tell that you didn't prepare for them specifically, they will feel betrayed and won't respond positively to your message.

Second, show respect for your audience. Don't insult your audience in any way. Racial slurs and profanity are obviously unethical, but in addition, don't show disrespect for people's backgrounds, positions, appearances, or nationalities. Don't put people down because of their ignorance of a topic; sometimes their ignorance is the very reason you have been asked to speak. Don't embarrass any member of your audience. Don't play a joke on anyone without seeking permission first. Even if you do receive permission, playing a joke on an audience member can backfire because the rest of your group might become fearful they will bear the brunt of your next joke, causing them to lose trust in you.

Third, base your conclusions in your presentation on clear evidence. Support your assertions with relevant facts, statistics, and testimony. Keep track of your sources and be ready to produce them if an audience member has a question. Don't make assertions you can't support or justify. Perelman and Olbrechts-Tyteca write in their book, *The New Rhetoric: A Treatise on Argumentation*, that whatever support you use should be able to satisfy the "universal audience," or that group of all reasonable, rational people.

Fourth, choose topics that are consistent with your personal beliefs. Pick topics important to you that you live out on a daily basis. You might be able to craft effective speeches advocating views you do not agree with, but you will be much more effective and ethical if you advocate opinions you actually hold.

Respect the time of your audience. Know what time you are expected to finish and finish at that time. It is an insult to your audience members and an abuse of your opportunity to speak to keep them ten, fifteen, or thirty minutes more than what is expected of you.

All of these ethical principles can be condensed to one, a "golden rule" of speaking ethics: Treat audience members as you would like to be treated if you were in their place.

ACTIONS SPEAK LOUDER:
MOTIVATING THE AUDIENCE

Sometimes in your presentations you want to motivate people to action or to change the way they think or believe. This requires different techniques from what you have learned thus far. It's one thing to help an audience to understand, but it's another step to move people to action. The best way to persuade people goes back to the Greeks.

Aristotle began it in *Rhetoric*, and others continued to write about three main categories of persuasion. The Greek words were logos, pathos, and ethos. Today, they are called logical arguments, emotional arguments, and speaker credibility. Despite the passing of twenty-three centuries, this three-fold division is still a useful way to consider elements of a persuasive speech.

Logical appeals deal with "hard facts" and drawing conclusions from these facts. Let's begin, then, with evidence. Included in evidence are facts. Facts can be demonstrated and observed by anyone. To say you are reading this part of the book is a fact. It's an event you can attest to and that can be observed.

Some facts are accepted on faith. Historical facts were, of course, one time observable and demonstrable, but now most of them have been accepted without that element of proof. That the year 1776 was a year of the American Revolution is historical fact, provable by documents, eyewitness accounts, and so on, but no one presently alive observed the events of that year.

One of the most significant ways to develop logical arguments is to show how what you are advocating works someplace else. In selling your audience on a new health plan, for example, if you can show the plan is already working with another similar company, this will have a positive impact on your audience. You often use this kind of support in casual conversation. You might say to a friend, "You ought to go to the Smokies for a hiking vacation. We did it this past fall, and it was a great time." You are saying it was great for you, and it will be great for them. Use the same approach in a speech. "This computer program worked great with XYZ company, and it will also work for you."

Another way of incorporating logical arguments is to use testimony from experts the audience respects. This requires knowing the expertise of the audience members and whom they would respect as sources for evidence. One of the reasons presidents from both major parties will quote

Abraham Lincoln is that he has credibility with everyone. If you were speaking to a group of basketball coaches or players, quoting Dean Smith, Bobby Knight, or Rick Pitino would enhance the point you were making.

A final way of stressing the logical is to state your conclusions. This may seem obvious, but don't assume the audience will draw the same conclusions from your evidence that you do. Think about filling in the blank to the statement, "As a result of this presentation I want my audience to _____." State this not only in the conclusion but possibly after finishing one of your key reasons in the body of the presentation. Don't take any conclusion for granted as far as your audience is concerned. State it for them and be specific in telling them the point you have made from your evidence. If this part of the chapter were in the form of a presentation, you might say now, "Use these three techniques, and you will be more persuasive in your presentation."

Not only must you appeal to the intellect in the Greek approach, you must also relate to the heart through emotional appeals. You jog to stay healthy (self-preservation). You obey the law not only because you think it is right to do so, but also as a way of avoiding jail or prison (individual freedom). You work hard at your job not only because you think it is the right thing to do, but also because it might lead you to a higher wage (personal gain). You install security systems in your homes because you want to be protected (self-preservation). Some of the other most common appeals speakers use include:

- Fear

- Freedom

- Love

- Patriotism

- Self-respect

- Sex

- Loyalty

- Hunger

- Pride

Emotional appeals are keys to moving people to action. Logical appeals can make audience members realize they ought to change their behaviors or beliefs, but it's the emotions that create movement in their lives. A speaker might give good reasons why listeners should give blood (logical), but the appeal becomes more powerful if the speaker refers to someone the audience knows who needs blood and how giving blood will help (emotional). The two must work together.

The third element the Greeks used, and one applicable for today, is ethical appeal. People are influenced by a speaker who has high credibility. This is simply the level of trust and confidence they have in what the speaker is saying. Here are a few of the factors that influence the audience's perception of your credibility as a speaker:

- The position you occupy

- Your reputation

- Your personal character

- Your knowledge of your subject

- Your sincerity

- Your appearance

- Your goodwill toward your audience

- Your skill in the delivery of your speech

How can you establish good credibility with your audience? To begin with, credibility has to be earned. It's not enough to tell your audience you know about your subject when your presentation reveals you don't, or that you have a fine moral character when members of the audience know that may be doubtful. But there are some things you can do to help establish your credibility.

First, what you say in your presentation can help establish credibility. References to your experience with the subject matter can help, as can references to your position, other audiences you have addressed, and so on. Be careful not to overstate your case, though, or you may end up with lowered credibility if your listeners see you as self-centered and self-important.

Second, seek to establish rapport with your audience. Let them know you care about them by what you say and use material that specifically relates to them.

Third, your skill as a speaker can influence your audience's perception of your credibility. You should be suitably dressed for the speaking occasion, show a concern for your audience, display sincerity in your style of speaking, and use appropriate language. In general, if you do an effective job of delivering the presentation, your audience will perceive you as a credible person. People form judgments about you from the minute they first see you until after you leave the room where you have spoken. It's important that you be fully and carefully prepared for the presentation and deliver it in the most effective way you can.

Obviously, persuasion takes place most effectively when logical argument and emotional appeals are combined with strong speaker credibility. All three are necessary. And in some ways they are interconnected. To tell an audience you are going to support your argument with evidence and logic, for example, might have a positive effect on them in terms of your credibility. At the same time, it may act as an emotional appeal—that you consider them intelligent and wise enough to understand evidence and logic. Careful attention to each of these sources of persuasion and to the ways they interact with each other can strengthen the persuasive impact of you and your argument.

You can certainly organize the persuasive presentation as you would an informative presentation, but an organizational pattern that is especially adapted to persuasive techniques is that developed by persuasion scholar Alan Monroe. The motivated sequence consists of:

- **Attention step** — Securing audience attention to the subject.

- **Need step** — Demonstrating a need for your proposal.

- **Satisfaction step** — Laying out your proposal as a way of resolving the need.

- **Visualization step** — Describing the future if the proposal is adopted or if it's not adopted (or a combination of the two).

- **Action step** — Setting forth precisely what you want your audience to do.

To sum up, Monroe's persuasive structure features three essentials in organizing material for a persuasive presentation: gaining immediate and purposeful attention, showing how your proposal satisfies a perceived need, and describing a specific course of belief formulation or overt action for the audience to take. Whatever organizational pattern you use, effective persuasion is most likely to take place when you give good reasons, appeal to people's emotions, and demonstrate your credibility.

Q AND A

SHOULD NOT MEAN
"QUIVERING AND AGITATED"

———◆·◆·◆———

"No question is so difficult to answer as that to which the answer is obvious."

—George Bernard Shaw

One of the most challenging and yet most valuable parts of a presentation is the question and answer period, which usually occurs at the end of the speech. Speakers often feel very vulnerable in question and answer sessions, but they don't have to. In the Q&A, speakers can clarify anything that confused people, and if handled well, speakers can increase their credibility through their ability to competently field questions.

Some people, of course, will take a question and answer session *too* casually. A famous scientist was often called upon to give his signature lecture, and he had a chauffeur who drove him to his engagements. The chauffeur would always come in, sit at the back, and listen. One day, the scientist was speaking at a place where no one had ever seen him before, so the chauffeur proposed a switch. "Why don't we trade clothing," the chauffeur said, "and I'll deliver your lecture? I've heard it enough times I feel pretty confident that I can give it as well as you can!" The scientist agreed to the switch. The chauffeur did a brilliant job while the scientist sat in the back of the room in the chauffeur's uniform. After he concluded, however, there was time for questions and answers. The first question was highly technical, and, of course, the chauffeur had no idea what to say. Without missing a beat, however, he simply said, "That question is so elementary I think I'll allow my chauffeur to answer it!"

In addition to clarifying things for your audience, the question and answer period adds value by reinforcing the key points of your presentation while receiving valuable feedback about the comprehensiveness of your presentation and any gaps you will need to fill in the next time. Two keys to handling the question and answer session successfully are encouraging questions and maintaining control.

A question and answer session without questions will be considered less than successful, so it's critical to encourage questions so that you have an opportunity to accomplish all the good things that can happen in a Q&A. To prompt good questions, first let the audience know early in the presentation that you will take questions after your speech. People are more likely to ask questions if you tell them up front that they will have the opportunity to do so later. In addition, they will listen more closely if they know they can ask questions at the end.

Second, ask for questions in a positive way. Ask, "Who has the first question?" Look expectant after asking the question, with your hands gesturing towards the audience and a smile on your face as you await a query. By asking this question, instead of, "Are there any questions?" you indicate that you expect multiple questions and stand ready to consider them.

But what if you get no questions after waiting a few seconds? You can still salvage your Q&A session by asking yourself a question to "prime the pump." Say, "A question I'm often asked is...," or, "A question some of you might have is...." For example, during a speech on public speaking a question Steve asks himself is, "Steve, in your opinion, who is the best public speaker among Presidents in this century?" Then he answers the question. This often stimulates curiosity among members of the audience and prompts other questions. But even if you have no questions after you finish your answer, you have had one question and answer, just as a Q&A requires, and you can sit down. Having no questions takes the edge off your presentation, as though your topic were not interesting enough for questions. But "priming the pump" either motivates other questions or allows you at least a basic question and answer period.

Another technique that encourages questions is waiting until the questioner finishes speaking before you start to answer. This sounds elementary, but it's very easy to anticipate the end of a question and go ahead and start to answer, interrupting the questioner. Even if you are right about how the question will end, your abruptness might easily discourage someone else from speaking up. It is amazing that anyone calls some radio talk show hosts because they only allow their callers about four words before they start interjecting their own ideas!

Keeping your answers concise also encourages more questions. From a strictly logistical standpoint, the more time you take to answer a question, the less time will be left for others to ask questions. Short answers allow you to respond to more people and make the Q&A more complete. Also, the ability to field several questions increases your credibility. Don't give another speech with your answer. If you can answer a question with "yes" or "no," then do so. This keeps the tempo moving and keeps the audience's attention. The only person interested in your answer might be the person who asked the question, so if your answer is brief, you won't lose everyone else. Thirty seconds should be a maximum time to answer most questions. If the answer will take longer than that, you might offer an abbreviated answer and then say to the questioner, "I'll be glad to talk to you about it some more after the session is over." If you have a hard time coming up with concise answers when you are put on the spot, anticipate questions ahead of time and practice brief answers. John F. Kennedy, who was very effective with handling questions at press conferences, would often spend several hours with his advisors before a press conference having them ask every possible question they thought might come up in the session. In this manner he was able to practice most answers before the questions were even asked by the press!

Another way to encourage questions is to recognize your own limitations—be willing to say, "I don't know." Many speakers are afraid to say, "I don't know," believing it will damage their credibility on the subject. But if people know you will be honest with them and not improvise answers, they will be more willing to ask you tough questions that can ultimately improve your presentation. It is helpful after the "I don't know," to add, "...but you might ask [knowledgeable person]," or "...but I'll try to find out for you." If you fake an answer, however, audiences are likely to know you are making it up or at the very least sense your discomfort and be less likely to ask you something difficult. Saying "I don't know" not only doesn't diminish your credibility, it can actually *increase* it by making the answers you do give seem more definite.

Encouraging questions in these ways will help you have a lively Q&A. But, as you have probably experienced, some question and answer sessions get a bit TOO lively. Consequently, you need to maintain control of the situation. Any time you open your presentation for audience participation, you run the risk of losing control. Several general principles for maintaining control exist. Anticipate questions. Stop questions irrelevant to your topic and move on. Whatever you do, don't lose your temper as you respond to someone who is trying to make you look bad. Never let the audience see you sweat! As always, be sensitive to time expectations. If you have a thirty minute speech, the Q&A shouldn't last longer than another ten minutes. Be sure you aren't going beyond the time the program is expected to end. Beyond these general principles are several other specific techniques for mastering your Q&A.

Look at the person asking the question while that person speaks, and then repeat the question. This gives you an extra few seconds to begin thinking about your answer, and it ensures that everyone has heard the question. It also ensures that you understand what the person has asked. If you paraphrase the question incorrectly, you will be able to tell from the questioner's nonverbal cues. Repeating the question is particularly important to maintain control in a large room, where some people might not hear the question or follow your answer. It's a good habit to develop regardless of where you speak.

After you have correctly repeated the question to the questioner, look at the whole audience as you answer the question. Remember you are in a public speaking situation, and the whole audience should hear your answer—not just the person who asked the question. We tend to give attention only to the person who asked the question because that is what we would do in a private conversation. But an answer in a Q&A is in reality a mini-speech directed to everyone. If you answer it looking only at the questioner, you leave the rest of the audience out and make people more likely to begin talking or not paying attention. As you finish answering the question, look back to the original questioner to see by that person's nonverbals whether you have answered the question satisfactorily and to acknowledge the person again for asking the question.

Another key to maintaining control is to defuse a loaded question before you answer it. No face-saving answer exists to a question like, "What are you doing with all the money you are making from increased prices?" So before you answer it, defuse it by stripping away the emotional implications of the question to find the core question you can answer. You might say, "I understand your frustration with the recent rate increase, and what you are really asking is, 'Why such a sudden increase in rates?'" Then answer that question. If you allow yourself to answer the loaded question, it will blow up into an argument. After you answer the defused question, if the person isn't satisfied with the changing of the loaded question's wording, say that you will be glad to talk about it following the question and answer period. Then move quickly to the next question. Even if you think you have a way to really zing your questioner, use this conservative approach anyway. You might show the questioner how he or she is wrong, but the audience will back the amateur communicator—the questioner in this case—and turn against the professional—you. You will be better served to defuse the question, reduce the tension, and help the questioner look good.

DEFUSING LOADED QUESTIONS

- Strip away the emotional words to find a question you can answer

- Say, "What you are *really* asking is..."

- Offer to speak with the questioner after the presentation

Sometimes questions aren't loaded at all, but empty—they are "non-questions." Cut these off politely. Some contributors to a Q&A only want to make speeches. To stop them and maintain control, watch their speaking rates carefully, and when they take a moment for a breath, interrupt with, "Thank you for your comment," and, "Who has the next question?" Look to the other side of the room and long-winded speakers aren't sure whether you interrupted or whether you thought the question/comment was really finished. Don't allow people to go too long, or their non-questions will ruin your question and answer period by keeping other members of the audience from asking questions. Knowing you will allow only questions will also keep the audience members paying attention.

You might also consider having your conclusion after the question and answer period. By pausing for Q&A and then finishing your presentation, you control the end of your time in front of the audience. Instead of the last question, the audience hears your prepared exit line. To introduce this kind of structure, say, "Before I make some concluding remarks, who has a question to ask?" Then when you have finished with questions, return to your conclusion.

The persuasive aspects of a presentation don't end when you finish your speech if you follow with an effective question and answer period. A question and answer period where the speaker encourages questions and maintains control tops off a solid presentation by adding the "icing on the cake!"

WHAT HAPPENS WHEN THE LIGHTS GO OUT

O ne of the greatest fears of speakers is not knowing what to do when things don't go as planned. A few years ago Steve spoke to about 300 people in an interior hotel conference room in Teaneck, New Jersey, in total darkness. A storm had knocked out the electricity. He could not operate an overhead projector, use a microphone, or even see the audience! When preparing for the presentation, he certainly had not expected to deliver it in the dark.

You might have prepared carefully for your presentation, but then just in the most important part, the room goes dark, the overhead projector bulb burns out, the slide projector jams, the temperature is so hot the audience starts going to sleep, or emergency vehicles passing outside begin to drown you out. What do you do? How does a speaker handle the unexpected? In Steve's situation, he moved closer to the audience so that people could hear him more easily—and so he could see them better. He mentally reorganized his materials to include his funniest and most stimulating stories first. He moved around the room to maintain audience attention. Then at the break, the lights came back on, and he returned to the material (and overheads) he had bypassed.

You might never have to deal with a darkened room, but this chapter offers general principles to remember when things go wrong, followed by advice for some specific crisis situations.

First, if something goes wrong, don't panic. If two people are talking to each other, just ignore them. If people go to sleep, don't immediately try to wake them. In most unplanned situations, the first thing to do is nothing. Often, what seems to be an emergency in the making will take care of itself if you just leave it alone. A public address system making popping noises can clear up on its own without any direct attention from you. People's noses adjust to unusual odors in a room. Distractions sometimes just go away on their own.

Second, store away in your mind some ad libs to use in case of an emergency. A guest lecturer in a college class obviously had an ad lib worked out for latecomers. A student came in about twenty minutes after the class had started and walked right in front of the speaker to get to a seat. The speaker stopped, watched the student cross the room, and then said, "Can I get you anything? A glass of water? A pencil? A watch?" The class roared for a moment, but order was quickly restored with the speaker definitely in control.

In another case, imagine you get tongue-tied on a familiar word or phrase. You might say, "I just got my glasses fixed a few days ago, and now my tongue doesn't work." Not long ago, Steve was in the first part of a presentation and the transparencies on the screen were shaking because the floor under the overhead projector was vibrating. Since he planned to use about 25 transparencies, this became a big problem. It was hard to concentrate on the words of the transparencies because they were shaking so badly. He ignored the problem with the first three or four overheads. As he was doing so, he kept thinking of what to do. He would go over to the table on which the overhead was placed and surreptitiously push down on the table hoping to stabilize the machine. Nothing worked. Finally, he stopped and looked at the screen and at the audience and said, "Well, this is the first time the overhead projector is more nervous than I am." The audience laughed, and he was able to go on in spite of the problem. The next time you deal with a vibrating overhead, you are ready with an ad lib! In your idea book, write down what you think of under the pressure of the moment and store it in your memory bank for future use.

Third, be honest with your audience. If you forget something in your speech, simply say, "I forgot my place; give me a moment to look through my notes." If your throat dries up on you and you have trouble speaking, say, "Excuse me for a moment; I need a drink of water," or, "Could someone bring me a glass of water?" Don't try to fake it with your audience. People know when you aren't being forthright with them; not acknowledging your problem simply damages your credibility.

Fourth, don't depend too heavily on audio or visual aids. They should only *aid* you in explaining your key ideas; they shouldn't compose the bulk of your speech. In an emergency, be able to give your speech without them. Fifth, check out any presentation aids ahead of time. Make sure the electricity is on and all your equipment is in working order before you begin the presentation. Turn machines on and off so that you are familiar with specific pieces of equipment. Focus your overhead projector so that you don't have to work with the knob while an audience is watching. If there is a light source directly above the screen, try to have it eliminated. Tape electrical cords to the floor so that you won't trip over them. If you use a laser or a wireless microphone, make sure you have good batteries. Clear enough space so that you can move easily around the machine and table.

A critical general principle is to get to your speaking room early. This allows you to handle problems before the presentation begins. Common problems include strange noises, uncomfortable temperatures, unpleasant odors, or unworkable seating arrangements. Correcting these problems might involve talking to a maintenance person or even finding a different room. Most of the time, however, these problems can be corrected if you get to your room early.

With these principles in mind, let's look at some commonly faced speaking emergencies.

You forget what you want to say next. Usually you can feel a loss of memory coming on. Before you freeze, repeat what you have just said. Repetition is a valuable speaking tool anyway, and repeating yourself will jog your memory and get you over the hump most of the time. A minister used this advice when he felt himself forgetting just as he quoted the verse, "Behold, I come quickly!" He repeated it, but still didn't know what came next. One last time, he said, "Behold, I come quickly!" and he said it with such force that he stumbled off the platform into the lap of a woman in the front row. He apologized profusely, but she said, "Don't worry about it. You told me three times you were coming!" If repetition, as in this minister's case, doesn't help you, simply admit, "I have forgotten my place. Give me a minute to look at my notes." Then do what you need to do to get back on track. This might mean rearranging your notes or transparencies at the lectern, or it might even mean going back to your seat to find the material you have forgotten. But the audience will be patient and sympathetic because anyone can forget. In fact, you will probably create a bond with audience members when this happens because they know it could happen to them.

The audience loses interest. You notice some people going to sleep or showing signs of drowsiness. Do something different! If you are at the front of the room, move into the audience. Speak more loudly or more softly. If you have been giving technical information, tell a story. Ask your audience to refer to something in the outline. Go to a visual. If you are already using visuals when the attention drift happens, turn off your machine and talk to the audience. You might take a short break, or you might even end your presentation early.

You follow a bad introduction. Introductions are critical to the speaker and sometimes you get a poor one, but you have to follow whatever the introducer says about you. If the introducer mispronounces your name, don't correct the person, but soon after you begin, say your name in the context of your presentation. If Steve followed an introduction that called him "Stew," he might say, "Steve, give me some advice on how to handle hecklers." This gets your name pronounced correctly without calling undue attention to the introducer's error. If the introducer doesn't qualify you as an expert, make it clear early in the presentation that you are qualified. You might casually say early in your presentation, "In my fifteen years of counseling troubled teens, I have found..." If the introducer gives incorrect information, and it is not critical, ignore it (e.g., the year of your graduation) or correct it in the same way you would correct your name—include the corrected information as part of your presentation. If the introducer plays the role of comedian, don't try to compete, but stick to your agenda. Whatever the introducer does wrong, avoid drawing attention to it. Highlighting the mistakes of the introducer will usually take away from your presentation and cause the introducer to look bad.

As the speaker, you have more control over the success of your introduction if you type one out and give it to the introducer. Most introducers welcome a prepared introduction, and taking care of the introduction yourself helps you feel more confident it will go smoothly. You might even specify to the introducer that you want the introduction to be read exactly as you have written it because it leads into the beginning of your speech.

A loud noise occurs outside the room. This might be a lawn mower, a vacuum cleaner, emergency vehicles, or people laughing or talking in an adjacent room. Ignore the noise as long as you can. Within a few seconds, it might subside. If the noise continues, however, you might ask one of the local people to check on it for you. Mowing and vacuuming activities can generally be postponed if someone only asks the staff. Noises also create good places for one of your prepared ad libs, such as, "Is it I or is it one of you they are coming to take away?" If the noise causes fear or concern from the audience (e.g., a severe weather siren), find out what it is, and share that with audience members to put them at ease.

People talk among themselves. Don't do anything immediately because they might stop on their own. If they don't, look away at the other side of the room. During that time, peer pressure might exert an influence and make them stop. Next, you might try moving into the part of the room where the talkers are. Your presence might intimidate them from talking. One of these techniques usually works, but if your presentation includes a break, you have a further option: approach the talkers at the break and ask for their help in keeping things going smoothly in the program.

Visuals fail. Sometimes problems with visuals aren't very technical. For example, a screen that will not stay down—the catch mechanism is broken. The easiest way to fix this problem is to jam a piece of chalk or a pen in the place where the screen comes out; this will usually hold the screen in place. Other problems, however, are more technical and more difficult to fix quickly.

If you have a problem with your presentation software, your overhead goes out, or your video is not cued up where it needs to be, acknowledge your problem and move on. If the visual is only for emphasis, such as an outline of significant points, work without it. If it's something that helps illustrate a point, however, you have two options. If you are in a long presentation you might hope your equipment can be fixed at the break and try to return to the visuals later, or if there will be no break, you might simply summarize the content of the materials, make your point, and move on.

Problems are unpredictable, but you can have an attitude that predicts you can handle whatever challenges come your way. Plan for the unexpected, and when it happens, you will be able to cope as though you expected it all along!

"I DID NOT APPRECIATE YOUR LANGUAGE."

"Many a man's tongue broke his nose."
—Seamus McManus

I f someone ever comes up to you after a speech and says, "I did not appreciate your language," you can almost be certain that your message failed to reach at least one person. Common courtesy is a good reason to be sensitive in your choice of words, but an even better reason is if you offend someone with your language, you are highly unlikely to persuade that person with your presentation. Sensitive language obviously includes avoiding off-color humor or profanity, but today it includes much more than that as well. Following a few simple guidelines about language will help keep you from offending anyone during your presentation.

Racial slurs are clearly inappropriate. But so is calling attention to a person's race if it is irrelevant. Simply saying, "I was talking to a Hispanic man the other day who told me..." is inappropriate if the man's ethnic group has nothing to do with your story. To be consistent, you would need to *always* use a racial descriptor—"A white friend of mine...," "A black friend of mine...," etc. In almost all cases, you don't need to use a racial term at all. And if for some reason you must (if physical appearance is somehow relevant, as in the case of certain statistics), use the term the majority of people in a racial group prefer. This changes over time, sometimes rapidly, so you need to stay as current as possible. As an example of a 1996 guideline, a U. S. Department of Labor survey of tens of thousands of people found the overwhelming preferences of people in three large ethnic groups in America are the terms "white," "black," and "American Indian." Note that these are not all terms you might think of as "politically correct," but they were the terms preferred at that time. If you must describe someone's race, use preferred words.

Discussing gender presents other challenges. Again, slang terms about gender are clearly out of the question. But a very real problem area exists with occupational names. Terms such as "mailman," "foreman," "stewardess," and "waitress" indicate only one gender and don't accurately reflect the diversity of people who hold those jobs; even if you don't offend someone with these terms, you might distract them for an instant from your message. In correcting terms like these to reflect the fact that both men and women can work such jobs, resist the urge to simply tack "person" on the end of the existing term. It sounds artificial, and it draws attention away from your content to your word choice. Choose terms that sound normal without indicating a particular gender—"letter carrier" or "postal worker," "supervisor," "flight attendant," and "server" are all natural-sounding alternatives to the older terms. And if you are ever criticized, ask your critic what term would be better to use. If you are ever stumped yourself, consult a resource such as Rosalie Maggio's *The Bias-Free Word Finder*.

As with race, calling attention to gender when it's irrelevant is simply unnecessary and might be construed to be inappropriate. With gender, the practice is known as "marking"—you are calling attention to, or "marking," the fact of gender. Usually marking takes place concerning terms traditionally thought of as relating to either males or females. Referring to a "male nurse," "lady judge," "woman engineer," or "male secretary" exemplifies the kind of marking to avoid.

A final problem posed by gender is the problem of the unnamed third person. We often refer to an anonymous "someone," "anyone," or "somebody," and then refer to the person again. But what word can we use? The tendency is to say, "they," but then you have suddenly increased the number of people to more than one! That doesn't make sense. Before 1980, the accepted practice was to use "he" or "him," but heightened sensitivity to language has called that tradition into question. The safest solution to this problem (which also avoids getting tongue-tied saying "he or she" and "his or her") is to use plurals. Eliminate saying "someone" and and start saying "people." If you use a plural in the first place, you can refer to those people as "they" and "them" with no problem!

It certainly takes some extra effort to use language that is sensitive to men, women, and people of various ethnic groups. But if it causes your message to be seriously considered by more people, the extra effort is worth it. If people decide from something you say that you are prejudiced against them, they will be very hard to persuade.

SPECIFIC SPEAKING SITUATIONS

THE SPEECH OF
INTRODUCTION

———◦•◦———

Whenever you are asked to introduce a speaker, you are given a very important task; the speaker's success, particularly in the beginning of the presentation, is directly related to the quality of your speech of introduction. If the introduction is too long, the audience will be bored before the speaker ever begins. If it is unenthusiastic or overly enthusiastic, the speaker will suffer from the audience's expectations. If the introduction doesn't make clear the speaker's topic or its significance, the audience won't have a good reason to listen. Help a speaker's presentation sparkle from the outset by delivering a strong speech of introduction.

First, keep the introduction short. Introductions should last a *maximum* of two minutes and should be briefer if the speaker is well-known to the audience. The primary purpose of a speech of introduction is to qualify the speaker as an expert on the topic of the presentation. If the person is already accepted as an expert, the introduction can be less than a minute. The shortest introduction of all, in fact, is, "Ladies and gentlemen, the President of the United States." It is unnecessary to say the speaker is a former governor of Arkansas, or California, or Georgia, or a past head of the CIA.

Second, avoid platitudes such as, "This speaker needs no introduction," or, "Without further ado...." If the speaker needs no introduction, then why is there an introducer? And what exactly is "further ado?" Instead of these vague cliches, use language that describes what is actually going to happen. Say, "Our speaker will explain...," or, "Today's speaker will talk about...." Never describe the speaker as the greatest or the funniest or the best; superlatives about a speaker before the audience can make its own judgment can cause audience members to be suspicious of your praise and can put unnecessary pressure on the speaker. Base what you say on facts: "Our speaker is in much demand. She gives about fifty speeches each year on this topic."

SPEECH OF INTRODUCTION OUTLINE
SUBJECT + SIGNIFICANCE + SPEAKER

Third, outline the introduction using the subject/significance/speaker formula. Begin by telling the audience what subject the speaker will address: "Tonight we are going to

learn how to overcome stagefright in giving a presentation."
Next, emphasize why the audience should listen: "We have
all experienced butterflies in our stomachs. Our speaker is
going to give us techniques to control our anxieties while
speaking." Finally, tell about the speaker: "Over the past
twenty years as a professor and trainer, this speaker has
coached thousands of students and executives to control
their stagefright." This section about the speaker usually
composes the bulk of the introduction. Choose facts which
make the audience want to listen to this person. Leave off
parts of the resume that have nothing to do with the topic
to be discussed. The subject and significance of introductions will almost always be brief, but the speaker section
accounts for most of the introduction's length. How much
you include here determines whether the introduction lasts
two minutes or thirty seconds. If the speaker is familiar, you
have a responsibility to be brief. If the audience doesn't
know anything about the speaker, then you have a responsibility to qualify the speaker to the audience so that the
person has instant credibility.

Fourth, check unfamiliar pronunciations of names and
places with the speaker. Go to the speaker and practice,
obtaining approval for your pronunciation. Not only will
this avoid embarrassing moments if you mispronounce a
name, it will also give you confidence when you speak it.
Milton Eisenhower, at the time president of Johns Hopkins
University, was giving a speech in Pittsburgh. His introducer mistakenly called the school John Hopkins University, so when Eisenhower got up to speak, he said he was

glad to be speaking in Pittburgh. Mispronunciations are annoying and unprofessional, but checking in advance allows you as an introducer to avoid mistakes.

Fifth, bring the speaker to the audience in a positive manner. Mention the speaker's name as the last words you say. Say the name clearly and enthusiastically and begin the applause when you finish. Use a statement like, "Please join me in welcoming Chris Davis" (applause). Stay at the lectern until the speaker arrives, then back away, and return to your seat.

Using these techniques will get your speaker off to a great start. Prepare carefully to make sure the introduction goes well. The quality of your introduction affects the initial success of a fellow speaker's speech.

THE SPEECH OF WELCOME

———— ◦•◦•◦ ————

The status of the welcome speaker often reflects the status of an event. To a high-ranking group of people, a CEO or an association president will deliver the welcome presentation. If the meeting is less high-powered, a mid-level manager or committee chair might welcome the audience. Regardless of who has this responsibility, though, this special presentation sets the tone for the events and speakers that follow.

The speech of welcome is usually delivered at the beginning of a meeting, conference, or program, and its primary purpose is to produce orientation and anticipation—to make people feel comfortable with their surroundings and their schedule and to make them feel good about being there. Normally the speech is short—no more than three minutes in length.

If you give the speech of welcome, be pleasant—people won't feel happy to be there if you do not look happy to be there. Smile, look happy, and act excited about the program, meeting, or tour that is to come. The content of the speech of welcome should include three elements.

First, you should speak on behalf of the people you represent. If you are a part of an association, you might say, "We at the National Producers' Association welcome you to this convention." If you represent a company, you might begin, "On behalf of the Anderson Group, I welcome you to our plant." At this point, you might also tell the audience some unique characteristic about the organization that audience members might find interesting: "We produce over 3000 widgets a day at this operation."

Second, predict pleasant experiences. Emphasize that what happens next will be positive for audience members. "We are going to take you on a tour of our facilities that will help you understand your role here," or, "Our speakers today will share with you how you can stay on the cutting edge in your field."

Third, stress how you want to serve the audience members. Mention what you are doing to make the day or program comfortable for them. Perhaps you are serving a special dinner, having a special recreational event, or offering some kind of perk if the audience members attend certain sessions or fill out evaluations. Give an example of what you are doing to serve them and indicate your willingness to do whatever else you can to make audience members as comfortable as possible.

In performing these three elements of a speech of welcome, make sure to include the name of the group you are welcoming, and make them feel you really are glad they are present. If you are welcoming a student group, for instance, you might say, "To you National Merit Scholars, we are especially delighted to have you at our facility because we know you represent the upper echelon of high school students around the country."

If any speech is a "feel-good" speech, this is it. The speech of welcome is not a time for controversy and certainly not a time for long-windedness. Even if it's not delivered by the CEO, a great speech of welcome makes people feel at ease and helps them look forward to what is to come.

THE EULOGY

"Sometimes when one person is missing, the whole world seems depopulated."

—La Martine

One of the most important and yet difficult presentations is the eulogy. Because it is typically delivered so soon after someone close to you has died, the eulogy as a ceremonial presentation often involves strong emotions. Funerals today often include non-clergy speakers, so you might be called upon to deliver a eulogy even if you are not a minister. Many funerals include several short eulogies by friends of the deceased in addition to the funeral sermon. This special speaking situation has several requirements.

First, be sure you know your role in the service. Whom do you follow and what is expected of you? Are you the designated person to represent the company, neighborhood, or family, or are you one of several friends of the deceased who will speak? Keep your remarks related to the position you are expected to fill. Recently Steve witnessed someone called on to deliver a eulogy because she was a research associate of the deceased. In keeping with her role, she spoke of the deceased's love of research and how her connection to the deceased revolved around that shared work.

Second, be upbeat. Emphasize things that will comfort family and friends and leave people in the audience with positive memories. Perhaps the person had a great sense of humor, or showed tremendous compassion, or was devoted to her family, or remembered birthdays. Pick out a couple of these positive traits and then give personal examples illustrating these traits.

Third, keep it short. Generally, you should speak no longer than five minutes. Two or three traits with concise personal examples will fit this time frame. Unless you are clergy, there will usually be other speakers besides you; out of respect for the family members, a funeral should not be too long.

EULOGY TIPS

- Talk about the deceased's positive traits and offer personal examples.

- Know your role.

- Be brief.

- Control your emotions so that people can understand you.

- Find an apt closing line.

Fourth, choose examples that won't overwhelm you emotionally in remembering the deceased. In fact, practice your examples before the service so that you can control your emotions enough to get through the eulogy when you are actually in front of the group. Although there is nothing wrong with tears at a funeral, your emotions might surprise you unexpectedly and make it difficult for you to finish if you haven't chosen carefully and practiced.

Finally, conclude your eulogy with a line that encapsulates the life of the person you are remembering. This line might be a quotation from one of the person's favorite writers, a line from a favorite hymn, a line from the Bible, or simply something you heard the person say once which you think represents how the deceased would want to be remembered.

Earl Spencer delivered a eulogy for his sister, Princess Diana, that followed these guidelines and became one of the most famous eulogies of recent years. He made it clear that he represented the family; he praised Diana and shared examples of her compassion, and he stayed within his time constraints. Although he expressed frustration with the press, he controlled his emotions enough to complete the eulogy and comfort the Princes Willam and Harry without breaking down. He closed with this: "Above all, we give thanks for the life of a woman I am so proud to be able to call my sister; the unique, the complex, the extraordinary and irreplaceable Diana, whose beauty, both internal and external, will never be extinguished from our minds."

You're probably not related to royalty, but especially if you are known to be a competent speaker, you are likely to someday be called upon to deliver a eulogy. By using this brief formula, you can honor the deceased by reminding everyone of why that person was special.

THE TOAST

———•◆•———

An appropriate toast provides the perfect way to top off a social event, be it a wedding or a business dinner. A toast is a way to celebrate an important event or person with words, and it's an ancient custom. The practice of giving and receiving toasts was common among the Hebrews in Old Testament times. In Psalms 116:13, King David alludes to this tradition, writing, "I will take the cup of salvation and call on the name of the Lord."

The word "toast" for this practice originated with the Romans, who browned their coarse bread in a fire. When the bread became too hard to chew, they soaked it in wine. The meaning of "toast" expanded to include the drink in which the bread had been soaked and then the person in whose honor the drink was consumed.

An effective toast quickly gets to the point. Brevity, conciseness, and directness are critical. If you take more than two minutes, you have gone on too long.

Effective toasts are also prepared. You must have a toast in mind that would fit the type of occasion you are celebrating; making it up as you go does not always work well. Think carefully about your opening. "I propose a toast to Tom to celebrate his retirement." After such an opening, you might simply invoke a traditional toast such as this one from Ireland:

> May the road rise to meet you,
>
> May the wind be always at your back,
>
> The sun shine warm upon your face,
>
> The rain fall soft upon your fields,
>
> And until we meet again,
>
> May God hold you in the hollow of his hand.

John Egerton's toast demonstrates that the finest toasts are simple but eloquent. These qualities are difficult to achieve, but worth the effort.

> Cool breeze,
>
> Warm fire,
>
> Full moon,
>
> Easy chair,
>
> Empty plates,

Soft words,

Tall tales,

Short sips,

Long life.

It is also important to be yourself in a toast. Although you might examine other classic toasts, put your own thoughts into the content of your toast. Personalize it so that it has meaning for you and the object of the toast.

Consider the context of the toast. Is it easy for everyone to stand? Will it be awkward to interrupt people from eating or talking to conduct the toast? Seek to arrange people and surroundings so that the toast is a natural continuation of the festivities, and if the situation is not ideal, wait.

Always have clearly in mind the names of the person or people you are toasting. At one wedding, the best man, who was single, had been quite taken with the matron of honor, Eileen, a happily married woman. In toasting the bridal couple, Larry and Nancy, he stood and announced dramatically, "I propose a toast to Larry and Eileen, and may they have many happy years together." No one actually heard the end of his toast because of all the laughter.

Create a dramatic flourish as you end. You want people to know when you are finished. Raise your glass at the end of your toast, "clink" with a partner, and take a sip.

CLASSIC TOASTS

May you live all the days of your life.
—Jonathan Swift

May you live as long as you want
And may you never want as long as you live.
—Anonymous

I drink to the general joy of the whole table.
—William Shakespeare

Be not afraid of life.
Believe that life is worth living.
And your belief will help create the fact.
—William James

This is a personalized toast presented by a best man at his best friend's wedding:

I had the privilege of meeting Axel seven years ago when I was a sophomore, and he was a senior in high school in Fort Thomas, Kentucky. In those seven years that I've known Axel, I've been able to see him grow in many ways: physically, spiritually—I've even seen him grow to like country music. And all of us here tonight have witnessed the growth of either Beth or Axel in some respect. But tonight Axel has grown beyond me, grown beyond all of us, in fact, save she with whom he has chosen to grow for the rest of his life. It is this happy choice and this happy future which we toast tonight.

Axel and Beth, we offer you our continued friendship, but no longer will we be either friends of Beth or friends of Axel, but friends of Axel and Beth, for you are now a couple. May your love be more famed than Romeo and Juliet's, more spiritual than Aquila and Priscilla's, and more passionate than Heathcliff and Catherine's.

As we raise our glasses to you, we wish you love, laughter, and the Lord's richest blessings. May you live long and grow happy together.

You don't have to be the best man in order to dazzle a social gathering with your eloquence and wit. Robert Louis Stevenson said, "That man is a success who has lived well, laughed often, and loved much; who has gained the respect of intelligent men and the love of children; who has filled his niche and accomplished his task; who leaves the world better than he found it...." Plan ahead and follow the simple guidelines in this chapter, and your toasts will win you friends and admiration.

INDEX

To order products or find out more about programs on written and spoken communication, call Steve or Josh toll-free at (800) 727-6520, or return this form to:

Steve Boyd Presentations
31 Winston Hill
Ft. Thomas, KY 41075

I would like information about:
_____ Presentation skills workshops
_____ Business writing workshops
_____ Listening seminars
_____ Creativity seminars
_____ Humorous/motivational speeches

I would like to order:

_____ *Boyd's Benchmarks*	@ $11.00	_____
_____ "High Bid" cassette	@ $11.00	_____
_____ "The Power of the Spoken Word" 3-tape set	@ $26.00	_____
_____ Newsletter (1 year)	@ $11.00	_____
_____ *From Dull to Dynamic*	@ $21.00	_____

Postage included. Make check or money order payable to Steve Boyd Presentations.